**BRIAN
MOORE
AND
MARTIN
TYLER**

**THE BIG
MATCHES**

BRIAN MOORE AND MARTIN TYLER

THE BIG MATCHES

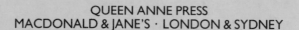

QUEEN ANNE PRESS
MACDONALD & JANE'S · LONDON & SYDNEY

First published in 1980 by
Queen Anne Press
Macdonald & Jane's Publishing Group Ltd.
Paulton House
8 Shepherdess Walk
London N1 7LW

ISBN 0 362 00501 X

Made by Lennard Books
31 Bedford Row
London WC1R 4HE

Editor Michael Leitch
Art Director David Pocknell
Designer Michael Cavers
Production Reynolds Clark Associates Ltd.
Printed and bound in Yugoslavia by
Mladinska Knjiga, Ljubljana

ACKNOWLEDGEMENTS

All Sport/Photographic 164, 165, 186; Associated Press 84, 92, 136, 138, 140, 158; Camera
Press 15; Central Press Photos 62; Colorsport 11, 68, 73, 76, 81, 82, 83, 86, 87, 89, 91, 95, 98,
135, 139, 142, 143, 146, 147, 155, 172, 173, 178, 179; Coton K. 103; Findus 14; Football
Association 14, 65; Griffiths B. 110; Keystone Press Agency 90, 145; London Express 16, 40;
London Weekend Television 85; Metson D. 104; Neighbour B. 110, 111; Popperfoto 22, 38,
120, 156, 157, 162, 163; Press Association 28, 37, 43, 44, 48, 56, 57, 78, 93, 96, 106, 148, 166;
S & G Press Agency 113, 161; Simon, Sven 119, 122, 123, 125, 127, 128; Sporting Pictures
66, 70, 74, 176; Staffordshire Sentinel 46, 51, 52, 53, 55, 56, 60, 61; Syndication International
12, 17, 20, 21, 22, 26, 31, 32, 34, 41, 42, 57, 94, 96, 100, 101, 130, 131, 132, 135, 170, 174, 175, 177,
180, 181, 182; Thomas B. 169; UPI 150, 157; Jacket illustration: Colorsport

Stoke City v Manchester United programme supplied
by Stoke City Supporters Club (London, South and West)

Photographic Research by Bernard Neighbour (Sunday Times)

CONTENTS

Football in the '70s, as in any decade, is filled with memories and moments to take into old age. Nothing is believed to be as good as it used to be; but, when we come to turn into another century, we are sure that men will look back with a warm glow as they remember, for example, Liverpool's conquests in Europe, Brian Clough and the things he said and did, Arsenal and their League and Cup double and, not least, our growing awareness of the skills and craft of overseas players that added so much to our enjoyment. Those were the days!

In this book we have chosen a match from each year. It was not an easy task, and our choice is always open to argument. But, as two working journalists, we decided to pick matches that evoked a personal excitement for us as we travelled around the world at other people's expense.

We have not looked necessarily for a heavy significance in the action or the result, but simply for the feeling that we got as fans. To help us, we have tried to stir the memories of players and managers who were involved in some of the games–and to our surprise their memories sometimes betrayed them when set against the recorded facts!

When we came to investigate that marvellous series of Stoke-West Ham matches in the semi-finals of the 1972 Football League Cup, for example, Trevor Brooking failed to recall that West Ham had scored from a penalty in the first game as a prelude to that historic miss by Geoff Hurst from the spot in the second. And Tony Waddington, then manager of Stoke, had even forgotten where one of the replays had taken place! 'I'm sure we didn't play at Hillsborough,' he said. But they had.

And when it came to England's substitutions in that 1970 World Cup game against West Germany in Mexico, even Bobby Moore, so cool-headed about so much, got the sequence wrong. Like so many, he believed that Colin Bell had been brought on when the score was 2-0 to England. But Franz Beckenbauer's recall was crystal clear. 'Bell came on just after I had scored Germany's first goal,' he said. And he was right.

So perhaps we are also able to polish up a few dusty images of great footballing days in the '70s. Our thanks to all those who willingly turned their minds back through the years for us and provided our stories with a richer texture. And our thanks to you for wanting to be reminded of days of joy, days of despair and a decade that has been fun to record.

Before you start reading the book I (Brian Moore) should explain the mechanisms of our co-authorship. For hours Martin Tyler and I sat over pots of coffee—and sometimes something stronger—waiting for the chords of our combined memories to hit a long-forgotten note.

We saw some of our selected matches together as journalistic observers but Martin helped cover the 1978 World Cup in Argentina for ITV while I kept the panel in order back in the London studio. So the account of Argentina v Peru is entirely his.

Likewise, I covered the 1976 European Championship Final and was close to Nottingham Forest for the 1978 European Cup Final. So those chapters are solely mine.

But together we hope you will think the idea is successful.

F.A. Cup Stolen

Chelsea deny theft, but say: 'The cup stays at Stamford Bridge!'

Both at Wembley and in the replay at Old Trafford they seemed likely to lose to Leeds. But in the first replayed FA Cup Final for 50 years they came from behind to win 2-1.

If territorial advantage counted for anything Leeds would have won at Wembley.

Time after time Eddie Gray rounded a bemused David Webb down the Leeds left. But the ball would not find its way into the Chelsea net. In Manchester it was the same story;

Jones scored for Leeds in the 36th minute, and for the next 44 minutes Bremner, Madeley, Giles, Cooper and company gave Chelsea a blistering time.

Then Peter Osgood sneaked a goal from a Cooke breakaway, extra-time was played and David Webb outjumped the Leeds defence to meet a long throw from Ian Hutchinson to nod the winner. Once again Leeds seemed to have been robbed of a certain trophy and the happy raiders from Chelsea carried the Cup back to London.

HOT SHOT GUNNERS! But can the Fairs Cup-winners rule the Home Front? See page 29

HOME CUP WINNERS

FA Cup Chelsea 2 Leeds 1 in replay after extra-time.
Football League Cup Manchester City 2, WBA 1.
Scottish FA Cup Aberdeen 3 Celtic 1
Scottish League Cup Celtic 1 St Johnstone 0

LEAGUE UPS AND DOWNS

Division I
Champions Everton, runners-up Leeds U. Relegated Sunderland, Sheffield Wed.
Division II
Champions Huddersfield, also promoted Blackpool. Relegated Preston, Aston Villa.
Division III
Champions Orient, also promoted Luton Town. Relegated Bournemouth, Southport, Barrow, Stockport.

Division IV
Champions, Chesterfield, also promoted Wrexham, Swansea, Port Vale. New admission Cambridge United were elected to the Football League and Bradford P.A. dropped out.
Scottish Division I
Champions Celtic, runners-up Rangers. Relegated Raith R, Partick T.
Division II
Champions Falkirk, also promoted Cowdenbeath.

BRAZIL'S FOUR GOAL FEAST...

WHILE THE REST of the world could only watch with admiration, the whole of Brazil celebrated as their national heroes cracked four goals past Italy in Mexico City to take the Jules Rimet trophy for the third time . . . and for keeps.

Architect of Brazil's 4-1 win was Pele. He started it all in the 17th minute when he soared gymnastically to meet a Rivelino cross. Later he laid off perfect passes for Jairzinho and captain Carlos Alberto to score.

Gerson, in midfield, was Brazil's other scorer. A defensive error, punished by Boninsegna, gave Italy her solitary goal.

Their message to the world on this day was joyously clear. Attack - and more attack!

Yet there was a period when Italy seemed to be about to haul themselves back into the match after going 1-0 down to Pele's

header. Their time of hope came after Clodoaldo boobed with a backheel in the 37th minute. Felix in the Brazil goal dashed off his line but Boninsegna poked the ball past him into an empty net.

For 20 minutes in the second half Italy hung on at 1-1. Then Gerson destroyed them with a glorious left-footed shot from outside the penalty area.

From that moment the match slid towards a rout as Brazil streamed forward in waves. In the 70th minute Pele pushed a short through ball to the feet of Jairzinho. He kept up his record of scoring in every one of the six rounds, bringing his personal World Cup tally to seven goals.

Four minutes from time Pele repeated the move for his galloping captain Carlos Alberto to hit goal no 4 past Albertosi.

HOME INTEREST in the European Cup centred first on the semi-final in which a brilliant Celtic twice beat Leeds, 1-0 away and 2-1 at home, to earn a Final place against Feyenoord. Celtic lacked lustre on the night but held out until extra-time when a goal by Kindvall made Feyenoord 2-1 winners. In the Cup-Winners' Cup, Manchester City were too sharp for Polish team Gornik, beating them 2-1 with goals from Mike Summerbee and a Francis Lee penalty.

The two-leg Final of the Fairs Cup was played between Arsenal and Anderlecht. In Brussels the home side took a 3-1 lead, but Arsenal showed they were a side with a future in the second leg, winning 3-0 to lift the trophy.

TRANSFER MARKET

MARTIN PETERS became Britain's first £200,000 footballer - taking over the top spot from Allan Clarke's £160,000 - in a transfer deal that took him from West Ham to Tottenham for £140,000 plus Jimmy Greaves.

Other deals in the £100,000 bracket took Terry Hennessy from Forest to Derby and John Toshack from Cardiff to Liverpool (both £110,000). Three others hit the century mark exactly: Peter Marinello (Hibernian to Arsenal), Alan Birchenall (Chelsea to Crystal Palace) and Dave Watson (Rotherham to Sunderland).

A more modest £20,000 changed hands when Phil Boyer went from York to Bournemouth. And Tony Hateley completed a personal circuit by rejoining Notts Co for £20,000. In eight seasons Hateley had been involved in switches costing a total of £400,000 as he moved from Notts Co to Aston Villa to Chelsea to Liverpool to Coventry to Birmingham and back to County.

Independent Television's darkened studio contrasted starkly with the glare of the Mexican sunshine. Within two hours, however, it would be totally in keeping with the gloom of the moment as England's traumatic day in Leon cast a shadow over the decade.

On 14 June in Leon England met West Germany in the quarter-finals of the 1970 World Cup. The kick-off was at midday. Back in England it was already early evening; and at the end of a sweltering summer's day the beaches had emptied quickly in the face of the live coverage of this re-match of the 1966 Final. The match was not the only topic of Sunday chit-chat. A General Election was only four days away and the candidates were kicking around their own political footballs. There are those who still believe that the score in Mexico greatly influenced the result at Westminster.

England entered the '70s as holders of the Jules Rimet Trophy, and automatic qualifiers for the 1970 finals. Eight of the winning side remained, with only the two full-backs, George Cohen and Ray Wilson, and striker Roger Hunt falling by the wayside through injury and the passing of the years. Alf Ramsey continued to hold the managerial reins – now 'Sir Alf' after receiving a knighthood among the rewards for guiding England to their first World Cup win.

Ramsey approached the Mexican campaign with the thoroughness of a battle-hardened general. The previous year England had toured South America, drawing with Mexico in the Aztec Stadium. With the 1969-70 season compressed to aid the international team, England were able to spend five weeks acclimatizing, including warm-up matches in Ecuador and Colombia. As our illustration overleaf shows, no chances were taken with the local diet. Stowed away on England's official flight were cases of food and bottles of drinking water. Special light-weight kit was introduced to combat the heat and altitude.

Ramsey maintained at the time that his squad was better than that of 1966, a feeling still endorsed by Bobby Moore, captain of both groups of players. Gordon Banks remained in goal, and would confirm his exceptional gifts by making the most remembered save of all World Cups from Pele in the group encounter with Brazil. Moore and Bobby Charlton, the core in the centre of defence and midfield – and world class performers in 1966 – were once again the side's fulcrum, though fears about the stamina of the 32-year-old Charlton were to influence the events in Leon.

Geoff Hurst, a shy hero of England's triumph, had drawn such confidence from his Wembley hat-trick to become a splendid example of the contemporary attacker. His former West Ham colleague, Martin Peters, had become the first £200,000 player in a transfer to Tottenham Hotspur in March 1970, and his superb technique and positional awareness marked him down as an outstanding international footballer. Alongside him in midfield Alan Ball, fiercely competitive and equally knowledgeable, was another automatic choice. Keith Newton of Everton and Terry Cooper of Leeds United held down the full-back positions, both energetic foragers in attack, an essential attribute in Ramsey's 4-4-2 formation in which they were asked to provide both quality and width. Brian Labone had solidly succeeded Jack Charlton at centre-half, while Alan Mullery brought greater all-round skills and no less enthusiasm to the aggressive midfield role occupied in 1966 by Nobby Stiles. The job of partnering Hurst in attack now went to

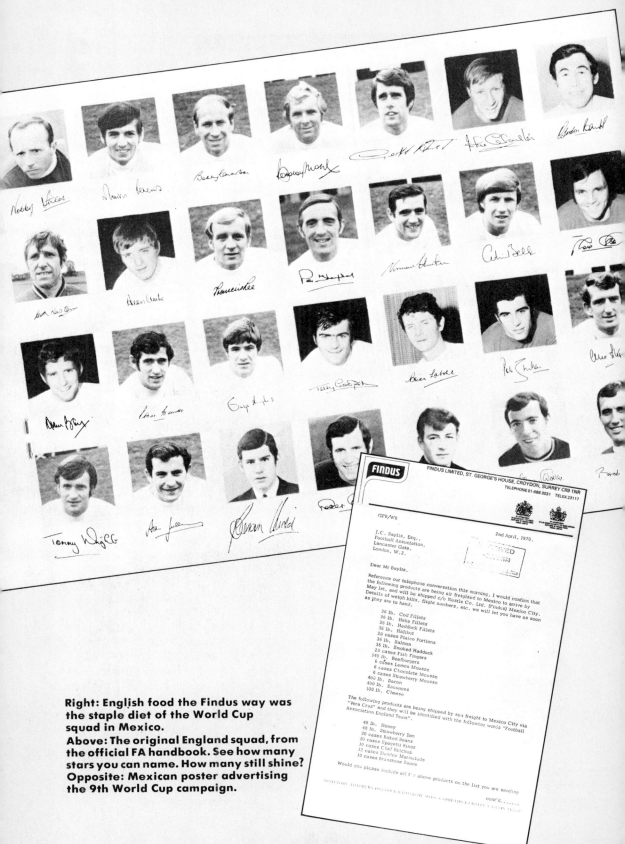

Right: English food the Findus way was the staple diet of the World Cup squad in Mexico.

Above: The original England squad, from the official FA handbook. See how many stars you can name. How many still shine?

Opposite: Mexican poster advertising the 9th World Cup campaign.

FINDUS

FINDUS LIMITED, ST. GEORGE'S HOUSE, CROYDON, SURREY CR9 1NR

TELEPHONE 01-686 3031   TELEX 23117

GFR/WB

2nd April, 1970.

J.C. Baylis, Esq.,
Football Association,
Lancaster Gate,
London, W.2.

Dear Mr Baylis,

Reference our telephone conversation this morning, I would confirm that the following products are being air freighted to Mexico to arrive by May 1st, and will be shipped c/o Nestle Co. Ltd. (Findus) Mexico City. Details of weigh bills, flight numbers, etc. we will let you have as soon as they are to hand.

```
36 lb.    Cod Fillets
36 lb.    Hake Fillets
36 lb.    Haddock Fillets
36 lb.    Halibut
20 cases  Plaice Portions
36 lb.    Salmon
36 lb.    Smoked Haddock
20 cases  Fish Fingers
140 lb.   Beefburgers
6 cases   Lemon Mousse
6 cases   Chocolate Mousse
6 cases   Strawberry Mousse
400 lb.   Bacon
400 lb.   Sausages
100 lb.   Cheese
```

The following products are being shipped by sea freight to Mexico City via "Vera Cruz" and they will be identified with the following words "Football Association England Team".

```
48 lb.    Honey
48 lb.    Strawberry Jam
30 cases  Baked Beans
10 cases  Spagetti Rings
10 cases  Chef Ketchup
12 cases  Dundee Marmalade
10 cases  Branstone Sauce
```

Would you please include all the above products on the list you are sending

cont'd.........

Manchester City's Francis Lee, who was a late arrival in Mexico, held back by an illness to his wife.

But Ramsey's plans, best-laid as they were, suffered in the way of the time-honoured phrase. His cold and unhelpful attempts at public relations, a continuing ache even to those journalists who knew him well, made England vastly unpopular in Mexico. His acidity at press-conferences was surely a defence-mechanism against those whom he mistrusted, but it did little to enhance England's image. His complete rejection of the local food cast his players as villains in the eyes of the Mexican fans. A further hiccup came with the infamous Bobby Moore 'bracelet' incident in Colombia which has been heavily documented in other publications, and which might have damaged the morale of the squad more drastically but for Moore's own renowned composure.

As in 1966 England began the competition unimpressively in their group base at Guadalajara. Hurst's name appeared on a World Cup scoresheet again, the only goal of an unspectacular game against Rumania. But there were far fewer deficiencies in the second match against Brazil, who were favoured along with England in the pre-tournament betting. The contest between the two countries who had won the three previous competitions lived up to its billing. England's efficiency under Ramsey provided a solid basis for their pattern of play. Brazil, with Pele back to full health, found only two genuine openings. From the first Banks confirmed his reputation with a breathtaking plunge to his right to flick Pele's perfectly placed downward header up and over the bar. From the second Tostao drew Moore out of the middle and Pele and Jairzinho profited from the space for the latter to score. England carved out chances to

equalize, notably those missed by Ball and Jeff Astle, substituting for Lee; but the substance in their play suggested that if the two teams were to meet again in the Final, as many experts predicted they would, the result would be no foregone conclusion.

Despite the set-back of their defeat, England secured their place in the quarter-finals when a side minus four regulars, whose energies were being conserved for later in the competition, contrived another 1-0 win over Czechoslovakia. Allan Clarke accepted the responsibility in his first international of taking and scoring from the penalty spot. But by finishing second in Group 3 England forfeited their own venue for the quarter-finals. West Germany had been based in the industrial town of Leon, 6,000 feet above sea level in a semi-desert area. England's hopes were to be ground into Leon's dust.

MEXICO 70
IX campeonato mundial de futbol
mayo 31 - junio 21

The troubles began before the team decamped in Guadalajara when Gordon Banks fell victim to a violent stomach pain. The vigilance of Neil Phillips, the team doctor, was such that to this day Banks himself is not wholly sure that the illness was an act of nature. The trumped-up charges against Moore in Colombia had induced a prevailing suspicion in the England party. To some the timing of Banks's attack was more than coincidence, though even to cynical minds the idea of deliberate poisoning still seems far-fetched.

England's illustrious goalkeeper was so weak that he could not carry his own baggage as the squad travelled to Leon, and yet he was not ruled out of the match until shortly before the team left for the stadium. Banks appeared to have overcome his discomfort as the players began their pre-match routine. But after breakfast he was forced to return to bed and Peter Bonetti was called up for the game that ended his international career.

Bobby Moore vouches for the lateness of Bonetti's call-up. 'When we got onto the bus to go to the ground, I thought Gordon was playing. He'd been

Alan Mullery glides the ball past Sepp Maier for the opening goal.

with us that morning and seemed better. Though we obviously rated him highly, we weren't greatly alarmed that he would not be with us. We knew that any member of our squad could come in and do a good job for the side. You have to remember that we were very confident at the time. Our morale was sky-high. We'd played so well against Brazil that we believed that we could win the World Cup again. And we knew that Brazil wouldn't have fancied playing us again. As for Italy, we certainly weren't worried about them. And of course we had a very good record in meetings with the Germans.'

It was not misplaced confidence because England began the match in such style that their subsequent defeat became even harder to comprehend. Controlling midfield with a superiority in numbers and ability, the side gave a perfect demonstration of the validity of Ramsey's system of play. To answer those critics of a selection that included only two recognized forwards, England displayed a mobility that saw midfield players and full-backs in advanced positions.

From one such move England confirmed their superiority on the half-hour. Cooper, who was well ahead on

The Ramsey method was seen at its best in the subtle crossfield build-up to the Mullery goal.

points in his personal battle with Libuda, robbed the winger again. The ball was switched, via Charlton, to Mullery, and then through a crossfield pass to Newton. Both players galloped forward, Newton with the ball and Mullery to meet it. When the right-back's cross swung deep into the German penalty area, Mullery got his reward, steering his first goal for his country past Maier.

From the same mould England fashioned a second goal which, coming five minutes into the second-half, seemed perfectly timed to finish off West Germany. Newton and Hurst combined down the right, once again freeing the full-back. This time the cross reached the far post where Peters played out his party-piece. His ability to outmanoeuvre markers off the ball by making late runs on their blind-side carried him clear and, from close range, scoring was a formality.

At 2-0 England's confidence upset Jack Charlton watching from the

stands. 'Instead of closing the game up and making sure we kept it at 2-0, our defenders were flying into their half of the field. It's not the way I would have done it. Sitting there I started to get very worried.' Ramsey, too, decided some action had to be taken and he ordered Colin Bell, a splendid athlete as well as a fine midfield player, to warm up with a view to taking over from Bobby Charlton. But as Bell, wearing a white Number 19 on his red shirt, loosened up along the touchline, England's relaxed air was shattered.

Beckenbauer's long silky stride carried him forward from midfield though Mullery forced him wide to his right. The defenders were almost urging him to shoot from an angle that favoured the goalkeeper. But when the shot came, low to Bonetti's right, it slipped under

Martin Peters steals in on the blind side of his marker. 2-0.

the goalkeeper's dive. There were 22 minutes of normal time remaining. Nine years after the event, Beckenbauer's recollections of the moment remained crystal clear.

'Everyone talks about Alf Ramsey wrongly making the substitutions, but you must remember that the substitutions came after I had scored my goal. It was not the substitutions but the goal which turned the game. At 2-0 we had no life. We had no air. At 2-1 we were given new air to breathe. I think Peter Bonetti was a brilliant goalkeeper but I believe he should have stopped my goal. Gordon Banks had the 'runs' didn't he? He might have stopped it, but who can tell?'

Bobby Moore carries the point even further. 'That goal certainly was

The fatal shot from Beckenbauer, wide to the right and out of picture, slides under Bonetti's dive. 2-1.

the making of the Germans in that game, but I also believe it was the making of Franz. He finally got out of Bobby Charlton's shadow. He always said that he never played well against Bobby because he made him run too much. He played as though he had handcuffs around his ankles and now they were removed. Not only did he score the goal, but in the next instant he found that Bobby was taken out of the game when Colin Bell came on.'

Ramsey, who admitted himself that he never felt easy about substitutions, decided to go through with the switch, and a bewildered Charlton walked off - for the last time in an international as it transpired. Both Moore and Alan Ball have gone on record as agreeing at the time that it was the correct move.

A spectator hoists the colours of the Bundesrepublik, and Schnellinger congratulates his captain.

Charlton's influence would be badly needed in the semi-final just three days away. His unceasing efforts in midfield inevitably made him more vulnerable to reaction against the sapping heat. With hindsight Moore offered an alternative view: 'It's easy to say now, but we really shouldn't have been so worried about Bobby. He was always very fit, and before the tournament started we held a mini-Olympics at our training camp. Bobby won most of the events.' Ramsey's move was further opened to criticism by the successful switch made by Helmut Schoen who, as in previous matches, had introduced a fresh winger at half-time. Grabowski had replaced Libuda and was now taunting Cooper down England's left.

Jack Charlton's sense of unease had by now reached such proportions that he could no longer bear to watch. 'I knew what was going to happen and I didn't want to see it.' He found a small cafe outside the stadium, and waited to watch for signs of the result on the faces of the spectators as they came out. He had longer to wait than he expected. He missed the frustration of a significant England attack. Hurst headed tantalizingly wide with Lee, apparently sure that the ball was going in, letting it pass in front of him. The cross had been supplied by Colin Bell in an energetic run down the right, and it is worth reflecting that had the goal been scored Ramsey's substitution would have been greeted as heroic.

As it was, he chose to make another alteration to his line-up. Seeking

Seeler leaps like an ageing but indefatigable salmon against Hunter. From another such leap the ball curved over Bonetti's head and sent the match into extra-time. Inset: Agony on the grass for England's deflated players as they prepare for extra-time.

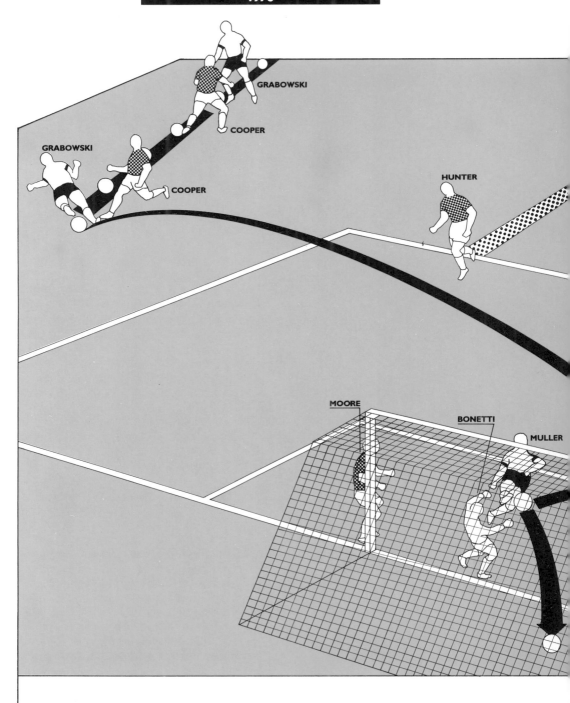

How West Germany made it to the semi-finals. From Grabowski the ball loops over to Lohr beyond the far post. Lohr heads it down to the deadly boot of Gerd Muller, who lashes it past Bonetti.

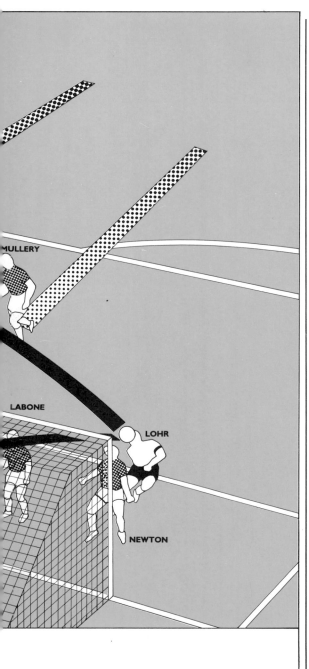

to protect Cooper against the waves of attack along his flank, he introduced Hunter, famously left-sided, to play in front of the left-back. Peters was withdrawn, but again perfectly sound tactical reasoning was immediately destroyed. West Germany equalized to send the game into extra-time where England would badly miss the creative skills of Peters and Charlton.

There was a cruelty, too, in the manner of the scoring. As Schnellinger arched a cross beyond England's far post the mind inside Seeler's head was surely striving simply to keep the ball in play. But the head itself guided the ball towards the goal and it dropped beyond a helpless Bonetti. England had survived a West German comeback in 1966, but then there had been a packed Wembley crowd to pump life into tired legs. Now, as the players awaited extra-time, all the psychological advantages belonged to Schoen's side. Bobby Moore remembers: 'Of course we were trying to be as competitive as possible but we had the feeling now that it was all going against us.'

England did not succumb to the prevailing tide without a fight. In the first period of extra-time they pressed forward but the balance of the side, so imposing in the game's first hour, had been lost in the substitutions. The misgivings of Jack Charlton finally became reality 10 minutes from time. Hunter's presence alongside Cooper could not prevent Grabowski taunting the full-back and crossing tellingly beyond the far post. Lohr leaped to head back across the goal, surely as Seeler had intended to do when he scored, and Muller applied the finishing touch.

England's grip on the World Cup had been shattered in a display that was totally out of keeping with their reputation. Even when they played badly they were never generous. Now for the first time under Ramsey they had lost a two-goal lead. For only the second time in 38 internationals since the 1966 triumph they had conceded three goals. At the final whistle the stupefied players exchanged shirts out of a sense of ritual, hardly recognizing which delighted German they were talking to. Ramsey, as tight-lipped and dignified in defeat as he had been in victory, congratulated Schoen before moving off to a bewildered dressing-room.

Bobby Moore retains a clear picture of the desolation. 'Alf was trying to console the players. Some were in tears.

Everywhere he was looking at blank faces with sunken eyes, and he must have been thinking, "What can I say to them?" Really the silence said it all. Everyone in their own mind was trying to work out what had happened. Though I have had some bad personal moments this was by far the worst in a team situation. Nobody could believe that we had lost. We had played brilliantly against Brazil and against West Germany – by far our two best performances of the competition. Yet we had lost both games.'

An exhausted West Germany finally went down to Italy in an equally

thrilling semi-final, fighting back from 3-1 down only to lose 4-3 in extra-time. The strain of that match on the Italians helped make Brazil's victory in the Final that much easier.

The frustration of Leon lingers because Ramsey's England of 1970 surely deserved to progress beyond the quarter-final, and arguably should have contested the Final against Brazil in a classic confrontation between the styles of Europe and South America. It lingers because it started the international decade on a decline. England were not to play another match in the World Cup finals in the '70s. Above all it lingers because it is a reminder that nothing in football is certain.

As the lights were switched on in our ITV studio for the members of the panel to find words to comment on the defeat, Malcolm Allison tore off his Union Jack tie and threw it to the floor. It was a gesture that brought some public reproach but it typified the mood of abject disappointment throughout the land.

Gerd Muller, the world's greatest finisher, scores West Germany's winner. This was the shot that started England's decline in World Cup affairs in the 1970s.

BLACK DAY AT IBROX!

66 killed, 200 injured

SOCCER-MAD GLASGOW was paralysed on 2 January 1971 by the shock of Britain's biggest-ever crowd disaster. In a hugely tragic human traffic accident, 66 fans were crushed to death and more than 200 injured at Ibrox Park just seconds before the end of a Rangers-Celtic derby.

The disaster took place when two opposing waves of fans collided on steep terracing at Rangers' home ground. Home fans were already pouring from the terraces as Rangers looked certain 0-1 losers. But suddenly Rangers equalised. When the roar of the spectators hit departing fans, hundreds of them turned and started to climb back for a view of the game's final seconds.

Moments later many lay trampled and lifeless beneath the even bigger main wave of fans now gushing towards the exits. When the terrible steamroller effect of the second wave had taken its toll, ambulancemen carried away an appalling total of 66 dead and dying. Around them the terracing was a battlefield littered with the moans of hundreds of injured.

Ibrox Park had seen crowd tragedies before, and the disasters of 1902 and 1961 were rapidly called to mind after that of 2 January 1971.
- During the 1902 Scotland v England match 25 spectators were crushed to death and over 500 injured.
- In 1961 crush barriers collapsed during another Rangers-Celtic derby, but the death-count was a more merciful two - though many more suffered injuries.

LEAGUE UPS AND DOWNS

Division I
Champions Arsenal, runners-up Leeds. Relegated Burnley, Blackpool.
Division II
Champions Leicester C, also promoted Sheffield U. Relegated Blackburn R, Bolton W.
Division III
Champions Preston, also promoted Fulham. Relegated Reading, Bury, Doncaster R, Gillingham.
Division IV
Champions Notts Co, also promoted Bournemouth, Oldham A, York C.
Scottish Division I
Champions Celtic, runners-up Aberdeen. Relegated St Mirren, Cowdenbeath.
Division II
Champions Partick T, also promoted East Fife.

HOME CUP WINNERS	
FA Cup Arsenal 2, Liverpool 1. **Football League Cup** Aston Villa 0, Tottenham H 2.	**Scottish FA Cup** Celtic 3, Rangers 1 after replay. **Scottish League Cup** Rangers 1, Celtic 0.

LEEDS AT LAST

DON REVIE and his Leeds United team at last became winners. They won the European Fairs Cup. But think what Leeds might have won in the last two seasons with just a pinch or two more luck.

In 1969-70 they stood to win everything - and ended up with nothing. Second in the League, runners-up in the FA Cup, and beaten semi-finalists in the European Cup.

This season had all the marks of the same nightmare. Arsenal pipped them in the League and Colchester humiliated them in the 5th round of the FA Cup.

In the end, the difference between being all-time losers and one of the best club sides in England - and possibly Europe -rested on the outcome of the Fairs Cup Final. Juventus of Italy were the opponents.

In the first leg, at Turin, Leeds managed to score twice in an exciting 2-2 draw. At Elland Road on 2nd June the home side again failed to win but the result - 1-1 - ensured victory for Leeds on the away goals rule.

WAY AHEAD of all rivals in the Football League was Ted MacDougall, who netted 49 for Bournemouth. His nearest competitor was Ray Crawford (Colchester U) with 32. In the top two divisions two players reached 30: Tony Brown for WBA and Malcolm MacDonald for Luton.

TRANSFER MARKET

AT £220,000, Alan Ball's move south from Everton to Arsenal was a British record. Other large sums changed hands for Malcolm Macdonald (Luton to Newcastle for £180,000) and Colin Todd (Sunderland to Derby for £170,000).

At Chelsea Peter Osgood was listed at £250,000 following a dispute with the club. Asa Hartford was ready to move to Leeds from WBA for £170,000, but the medical showed up a suspect heart condition and Leeds withdrew.

Lower down the list some interesting minnows were moving about. For £35,000 Kevin Keegan left Scunthorpe for Liverpool, and Middlesbrough paid Mansfield £50,000 for Stuart Boam. Meanwhile, Stan Bowles shuffled from Crewe to Carlisle.

NEWS IN BRIEF

■ 16-year-old Birmingham striker Trevor Francis scored four against Bolton.
■ Doncaster Rovers chairman said Lawrie MacMenemy must go.
■ Peter Bonetti played 500th game for Chelsea.
■ George Best fined a record £250 for keeping FA Disciplinary Committee waiting for 90 minutes.

In a decade of outstanding club achievements by the likes of Liverpool and Nottingham Forest, the accomplishment of Arsenal in 1971 still sets them apart. The much-acclaimed double of League Championship and FA Cup in the same season had been performed only in the formative years by Preston North End and Aston Villa, and in the more competitive modern environment by the marvellously gifted Tottenham Hotspur side of 1961. But on no occasion had it been done with the remarkable defiance of logic of Arsenal's dual triumph. And not, like Arsenal, in the same week.

At the end of January, Leeds United led the First Division by seven points, surely uncatchable in an era of functional football in which Don Revie's side gave away precious little. In the FA Cup Arsenal were drawn away in every round, with tasks varying from the threat of being toppled on Yeovil's sloping pitch to the First Division challenges of Manchester City and Leicester City. In the semi-final they trailed 2-0 to Stoke, and 2-1 inside the final minute. Yet they arrived at the final week of the season on course for that elusive double.

Persistence, skill – much of which went unappreciated at the time – and an unquenchable will to win lifted Arsenal from the periphery to the forefront in the race for honours. They were to prove to be the most organized at a time in the game's development when organization was a key factor. In manager Bertie Mee the club possessed a superb administrator whose professionalism commanded the respect of his staff. Don Howe, a coach with first class credentials, carried the attention to detail onto the field, producing a side vigilant in defence and effective, if not always subtle, in attack.

But, as Don Howe recalled, the side that was to write its name into the record books was not completely a product of planning: 'George Graham was recognized as a striker, but might well have been on his way to leaving the club when he went on as substitute at Tottenham before the double season. In the reshuffle he had to play in midfield, and he did so well that Bertie and I decided to keep him there for the next match at Coventry. We asked him if he was prepared to have a go. He did well in a sort of left-half position and never looked back. That was something of an accident that worked in our favour, and he established a marvellous understanding with George Armstrong.

'Then, in our first game of the year we did the double, Charlie George broke his ankle at Everton and didn't play again until the New Year. Ray Kennedy had scored an important goal for us in the Fairs Cup Final the previous season, but though he was doing well in the reserves he wasn't really pushing for a first-team place. But with Charlie's injury he had to be given an extended run, and he quickly linked so well with John Radford that he established himself.'

In goal Bob Wilson, once a schoolmaster in Chesterfield, and a late-entrant into top class football, was nearing the completion of the transition from being talented but inconsistent to a brave, safe 'keeper of international class. Frank McLintock, so creative in midfield, had made the switch to centre-half following the sale of Ian Ure to Manchester United, to link up with Peter Simpson. Don Howe was to pay tribute to the importance of his two central defenders. 'Both players had previously been in midfield and their skills served us well. Although we didn't get too much credit for it at the time, we played a lot of good football from the back.' Flanking McLintock and Simpson were Pat Rice, who had emerged from the youth team, and Bob McNab, purchased from Huddersfield Town.

Peter Storey was cast in the role of 'heavy' in midfield after breaking into the first team at right-back. A series of successful marking jobs on George Best had illustrated a defensive flexibility and the phlegmatic Storey was to succeed Nobby Stiles and Alan Mullery as England's ball-winner. But even in success Don Howe was never to be totally satisfied with the midfield blend. 'Storey and Graham did just what was required but we never quite got the right-sided midfield position sorted out. Eddie Kelly, Jon Sammels and later Charlie George all played there but without really making the job theirs.'

Up front Radford and the young Kennedy ran willingly in the team cause, with George Armstrong able to probe unceasingly down both flanks and still have the appetite to harass and chase back, a willingness that plugged any gaps caused by Graham's forays forward. If the overall style never totally captured the public's imagination they could not ignore it. As the 1970-71 season developed Arsenal simply went on winning and winning.

From 6 February to 20 April they won 11 out of 12 League games, nine successive victories following a 2-0 defeat at Derby. On 17 April they finally topped the table when Leeds lost at home to West Bromwich Albion, who had not won an away game for 16 months. Jeff Astle's winning goal, after Colin Suggett in a clear offside position had been judged not to be interfering with play, caused such furore among the Elland Road crowd that the club was subsequently banned from using the ground for four home matches at the start of the following season.

But controversy ran in Leeds's favour in their next home game against

Arsenal, when Jack Charlton scored the only goal. Again its validity was questioned on grounds of offside. Nevertheless with goal average an increasingly relevant factor, a continuation of Arsenal's winning ways would lead them to the Championship. Meanwhile in another act of brinkmanship Peter Storey had been an unlikely hero in keeping the club in the FA Cup. His shot through a crowded penalty area had cut Stoke's advantage in the second half, and in injury time he icily slid a penalty past Gordon Banks to ensure a replay. Stoke's chance had gone and Arsenal cantered through the replay at Villa Park, with goals from Kennedy and Graham, to meet Liverpool in the Final.

On Saturday 1 May Leeds won their last League match, at home to Nottingham Forest, but Arsenal again accounted for Stoke, a 1-0 victory that typified much of their season. It was their fifth win by such a margin in 10 games. At last the League was there for the taking. A win in their final League game would guarantee the title. A goalless draw would also suffice, but with the intricacies of goal average, a scoring draw would take the Championship to Elland Road. All the drama was heightened by a further quirk of fate: the last match was away to Tottenham Hotspur, Arsenal's most earnest rivals, on the following Monday.

As pulses quickened throughout North London, Don Howe recalls surprising calmness at Highbury as the club set out on its historic week: 'We'd kept telling the players we would win the double, but we really didn't think so. So that when we had beaten Stoke in the

Charlie George, the idiosyncratic striker whose shooting power carried the day at Wembley in the climax of Arsenal's great week.

League it was the first time that we really came face to face with the prospect. There had been no build-up of pressure. There wasn't time to get all tensed up.

'In fact the players came off the field looking drawn and tired at the end of a long season, but rarely has a team had such ambition for success. If there was any suspicion of tension, the old heads like McLintock and Graham kept it under check.'

Mee and Howe saw no reason to change their routine and Sunday was the usual rest day, with the squad reporting for light training on the morning of the Monday match. But they were without Peter Storey who had a recurring groin strain which would keep his Cup Final place in doubt for the entire week. Luckily Kelly, who was substituting for Storey when he scored the winning goal against Stoke, was a steady replacement.

The players lunched at home before re-assembling at 4.30 pm at their regular pre-match rendezvous, the South Herts Golf Club – by which time many of an estimated 150,000 had set out for White Hart Lane. Bertie Mee was already aware of the fervour. 'We gave ourselves an hour for a drive that normally takes twenty minutes. But even then it was a very difficult journey. I have never seen scenes like it. The coach crawled towards the ground even with our police escort. But there was never the pressure that we were going to be late, and seeing those thronging crowds increased the sense of occasion for us. There was no way we were going to be beaten.'

But no team would delight more

in stopping the Arsenal march than Spurs who would have to live at close quarters with their rivals' success. Leeds United, meanwhile, awaited their fate at Hull where they were providing the opposition for a testimonial match.

More than an hour before the kick-off the gates were closed behind 51,192 fortunate spectators crammed inside White Hart Lane, and in the faces of another hundred thousand outside, many of whom stayed to follow the ebb and flow of the game through the cheers. On the field Frank McLintock found those cheers a handicap. 'I kept shouting advice and instructions to try to keep on top of things but I might as well have been talking to myself. You just couldn't hear a thing out there. The noise was deafening.' But any nerves were kept in check by a calm, measured Arsenal performance – though it was not without its scares.

Martin Peters clipped the Arsenal bar with a curving shot. Wilson was hurt performing what had become his party-piece, a spectacular dive at the feet of an opponent, this time Joe Kinnear. Alan Gilzean took his eye off the ball when it seemed that he must convert a cross from Cyril Knowles.

In the stand Bertie Mee sat alongside Dennis Hill-Wood. Arsenal had won the Fairs Cup the previous season, their first trophy for 17 years, but both manager and chairman had their hearts set on the League title. On the bench Don Howe viewed the match with as much professional detachment as he could muster. 'There were a few scares early on, but I never felt we were in real trouble. We had worked on containing Martin Chivers, and our back four looked solid. It looked all over like a no-goals draw.'

Three minutes from the end Arsenal iced their cake. Spurs struggled to

George Graham heads for the Spurs goal, with Martin Peters a grounded spectator. The score was still 0–0. Inset: It's in! Kennedy's 87th-minute header crosses the Spurs line. 0-1.

clear a John Radford header and when Armstrong played the ball back into the middle, Kennedy scored with a joyous header. Even then, had Spurs been stung into an equalizer, the title would have gone to Leeds! But when Kevin Howley blew the final whistle the Arsenal fans swept on to the pitch in a gesture of celebration that brought severe problems to their heroes.

Don Howe hardly had time to savour the moment of success. 'My thoughts turned straight to the Cup Final and I was worried that the crowd might injure our players. They were ripping at their shirts. Some wanted their boots which of course they had to wear on Saturday. I was frightened that they would tread on someone's foot and keep him out of the Final.

'After twenty minutes some of the players had still not made it back to the dressing-room and we pleaded with the police to go out on to the pitch to rescue them. But they said that if the lads couldn't get off how could the policemen get on. We then asked them to send on the horses but I think they were reluctant to do that in case they damaged the pitch! But thank goodness, no one was injured and all that went missing was a few shirts.'

Missing, too, was Bertie Mee's club tie, grasped as a souvenir as he returned to the directors' box to acknowledge the applause of the crowd, and in reflection he acknowledges the generosity of his hosts on the night: 'Bill Nicholson brought us in champagne and Spurs threw open their hospitality rooms on our behalf. There had been an awful lot of bad feeling between the two clubs in the past but I like to think I helped break that down. I am sure they were dis-

34

appointed that they hadn't beaten us but they entertained us marvellously after the match.'

Even with a Cup Final only five days away the players carried on their celebrations late into the night at a private party in the White Hart public house in Southgate. The Arsenal management placed no restriction, said Howe. 'We believed it was better for the players to fully unwind and they had the Tuesday off to recover. There was plenty to celebrate too because in all honesty we felt we had to win the League because we had a nagging doubt about our ability to win at Wembley. We all had bitter memories of our two League Cup Final defeats against Leeds and Swindon.'

Now with the impetus of the Championship behind them Arsenal set out to lay that Wembley bogey. At their training ground in London Colney a luxurious pitch had been given special treatment. The grass was allowed to grow to give a Wembley feel to the turf, and the dimensions were altered to conform in every detail with that of the Empire Stadium playing area. As the players regrouped on the Wednesday, they faced the barrage of media coverage that is both a financial bonus and potential distraction to Cup finalists. But for the representatives of the press, radio and television it was a short period of

The strange taste of success: match-winner Ray Kennedy is anointed at White Hart Lane with a double bitter lemon. Now Arsenal could fix their minds on the Cup Final.

access. Bertie Mee was adamant:

'After Thursday I put a complete block on media involvement. I wanted to protect the players from outside pressures. I told them to take their phones off the hook or to get someone else to answer them. I was adamant about this. And I firmly believe still that this is the way to approach a Final. Liverpool were heavily involved in matters of publicity and though Bill Shankly would always tell you his side were the fittest in the League, four or five of his players went down with cramp at Wembley. None of our players did. And though cramp is partially a matter of fitness, there is a tremendous emotional overlay as well.'

Even the manager's carefully gauged planning offered no protection against superstition. Following their failure in the two League Cup Finals, of 1968 and 1969, Arsenal altered their pre-match hotel location to the Grosvenor House in Park Lane (where they were also to stay prior to their 1979 FA Cup win over Manchester United). As Don Howe arrived on the Friday the hall porter told him that West Bromwich Albion had placed the Cup on his table three years earlier. 'We'll bring it back for you tomorrow,' said Arsenal's coach in a light-hearted moment of bravado.

The superstitions continued into the morning of the Final. Before their two recent Wembley defeats the party had departed from their traditional visits to the South Herts Golf Club. Not this time. So, instead of the usual morning lie-in, by ten o'clock Arsenal were on their way to familiar haunts. There Dai Rees, the resident professional, exhorted the players to believe in victory with his own brand of optimism that had led to stirring Ryder Cup exploits.

Arsenal had taken a gamble on Storey's fitness though he was not to last out the Final. Slotting into their pattern of play in which the strength and aggression of Radford and Kennedy gave the rest of the side a focal point, Arsenal began confidently. Kennedy might have scored. Armstrong should have when he failed from close-in, almost under the very crossbar.

Liverpool, who brought on Peter Thompson for Alun Evans mid-way through the second-half to give their attack more variety, still could not find a meaningful retort of their own, and a generally disappointing 90 minutes finished goalless. But after only six

Steve Heighway clenches his fists after sliding in Liverpool's goal. 0–1.

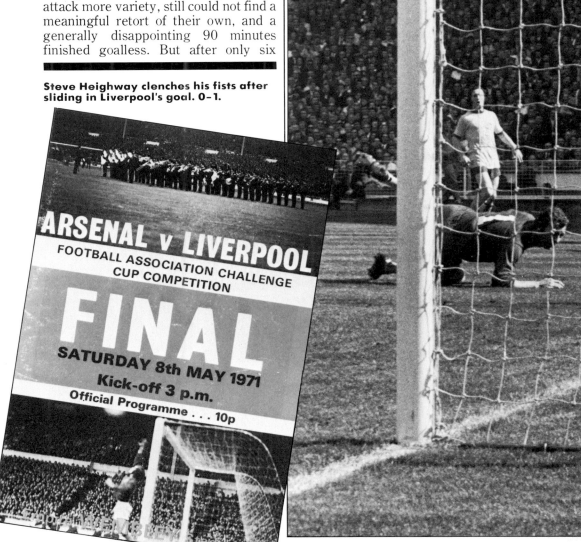

ARSENAL v LIVERPOOL

FOOTBALL ASSOCIATION CHALLENGE CUP COMPETITION

FINAL

SATURDAY 8th MAY 1971
Kick-off 3 p.m.

Official Programme . . . 10p

minutes of extra-time, Steve Heighway, making an astonishing impact as a leggy coltish winger in his first season, cut in from the left. Wilson anticipated a cross but Heighway drove his shot in at the near post from a tight angle. No fluke, he had scored in identical fashion in a Merseyside derby earlier in the season.

Don Howe vividly recalls his reaction on the Arsenal bench: 'First of all I thought, well we've won the League and we've not had a bad old season, but of course my next reaction was to do something about getting a goal. Charlie George hadn't played very well, and he was nearly out on his feet in the heat. But we'd already put Eddie Kelly on for Storey. So I decided to throw George

Graham forward and drop Charlie back into midfield, and I told George Wright, our physio, to get down on the line to pass on the message.' Immediately the word got through, Graham's strength caused confusion close to Ray Clemence's goal, and the tall, elegant man, nick-named 'Stroller', wheeled away in triumph believing he had got the final touch to Arsenal's equalizer. The following day ITV's cameras would show conclusively that Eddie Kelly, who had knocked the last pass into the goal area, was tech-nically the scorer. But Howe's move had

George Graham takes a swing at the ball but the real scorer was Eddie Kelly, following up behind. 1–1.

worked. Now it was time for another re-think.

'Once we had equalized I settled for the draw. It had not been our day overall, and I felt that it would be better to steady ourselves and start out afresh for the replay. I decided to get George Graham back into midfield just to make sure he got behind the ball. Charlie still looked knackered, so I wanted him back up front. Out of the way really. I sent George Wright down again to make the switch. It really was a defensive move.'

That was how, in the second half of extra-time, Charlie George came to be hovering outside the Liverpool penalty area. George's shooting power was un-questioned, and his 20-yard shot flashed past Clemence to the goalkeeper's right. Now he dropped to the ground, flat on his back, waiting for congratulation – a gesture interpreted at the time as in keeping with his idiosyncratic character but in reality a reaction to his exhaustion. He was simply too tired to run to the crowd for a conventional salute.

Arsenal's season had been all about staying in front when they got ahead, and they withstood the final, desperate Liverpool attacks. Yet there was inescapable irony that in a season of superb planning the winning goal had come in spite of the tactics! Frank McLintock, a four-time Wembley loser, finally savoured the taste of victory as he collected the Cup. The double was complete.

Why were Arsenal so invincible that season? Bertie Mee recalled: 'We were well organized and we had a lot more skill than people gave us credit for. And our morale was unsurpassed. The players appreciated each other's weaknesses and would compensate for them. And they were also able to play to each other's strengths. The chemistry both on the field and off it was just right. Previously the team had travelled in Europe together and our experiences in Rome against Lazio and places like Rumania forged a bond. And of course all the players had a tremendous respect for Don who is a first-class coach. It was my job to plan and to pay attention to detail and let Don and the players get on with their job. My job was to take the pressure and keep it from getting to them.'

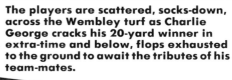

The players are scattered, socks-down, across the Wembley turf as Charlie George cracks his 20-yard winner in extra-time and below, flops exhausted to the ground to await the tributes of his team-mates.

Howe himself paid tribute to a winning attitude: 'They all had this winning streak. It showed out even in team meetings. I lived next door but one to Frank McLintock and we would travel to training together. Sometimes I would warn him that I was going to have a real go at him in the team talk. And that would set off the most brutally honest discussions. Nothing was held back. Everyone took the criticism and then would give some back. I felt almost sadistic at times bringing it out of them, even those like Bob Wilson who initially did not take too kindly to criticism and Charlie who in another dressing-room might have sat quietly through it. After-

wards they would all march out with an "I'll show you" attitude. Some of our five-a-side games became so frightening I had to stop them!

'And though I handled the players, Bertie's influence was all-important. When he said jump they jumped. If I felt a little below par at training, and every-one has days like that, Bertie would be there. He'd stop training and demand more effort. And he always got it. If any of the lads answered back he always had quick replies to assert his authority.'

Bob McNab was to say later that

Frank McLintock at Wembley and, opposite, on the Town Hall steps next day.

Arsenal should have repeated their double the following season: 'It would have been easier having done it once.' But they were to fall heavily between the two stools, losing in the Cup Final to Leeds and coming second in the League behind Brian Clough's Derby County. All the players remained, reinforced by Alan Ball, but Howe had gone, within weeks of the double, to manage West Bromwich Albion.

'Everybody thought I left because I wanted Bertie's job, but that wasn't so. I did want to manage in my own right. But I wasn't in a hurry. Being manager of Arsenal is still my ambition but I would have been prepared to wait, four, five, ten years if necessary. All it would have taken to keep me at Highbury would have been a promise that when Bertie decided to finish I would be given a go as manager for a year or two years. But nobody said that.'

Don Howe spent four years at Albion before coaching at Leeds. But he finished the decade back at Highbury as right-hand man to Terry Neill. Bertie Mee left Arsenal in 1976 and later Watford called for his experience to assist Graham Taylor, their young manager. In 1979 Watford won promotion back to the Second Division, and Arsenal lifted the Cup. That winning attitude lived on.

It's Derby

The most amazing four-horse race for the League title ended with all runners gasping for breath — except for Derby. They completed their programme and waited on a Spanish beach while the other three contenders - Leeds, Liverpool and Manchester City - battled down the home stretch towards their total of 58 points.

Manchester City blew up first, and could only finish with 57. But by Cup Final day the other two were in with a chance. In the end it all hung on what Leeds and Liverpool could do on the Monday night after the Cup Final.

Leeds, themselves in the Cup Final, had to go to Wolves, and Liverpool were booked to face Leeds' opponents in the Cup Final, Arsenal, away at Highbury.

On the Saturday, Leeds carried off the Cup with a 1-0 win and hurried north to prepare for Monday night's decider. A draw would give them the title. They played . . . and lost 2-1, a goal by Derek Dougan nailing their hopes of the Double.

At Highbury, Arsenal shut out Liverpool 0-0 — and millions of home mathematicians saluted a fresh name at the head of the League — Derby County.

As a reminder of how close it was, take a look at the final League table, below.

				Home			Away				
	P	W	D	L	F	A	W	D	L	F	A	Pts
Derby Co	42	16	4	1	43	10	8	6	7	26	23	58
Leeds U	42	17	4	0	54	10	7	5	9	19	21	57
Liverpool	42	17	3	1	48	16	7	6	8	16	14	57
Man City	42	16	3	2	48	15	7	8	6	29	30	57
Arsenal	42	15	2	4	36	13	7	6	8	22	27	52

LEAGUE UPS AND DOWNS

Division I Champions Derby Co, runners-up Leeds. Relegated Huddersfield T, Nottingham F.
Division II Champions Norwich C, also promoted Birmingham C. Relegated Charlton A, Watford.
Division III Champions Aston Villa, also promoted Brighton. Relegated Mansfield T, Barnsley, Torquay U, Bradford C.
Division IV Champions Grimsby T, also promoted Southend U, Brentford, Scunthorpe U. Hereford U elected to League in place of Barrow.
Scottish Division I Champions Celtic, runners-up Aberdeen. Relegated Clyde, Dunfermline.
Division II Champions Dumbarton, also promoted Arbroath.

HOME CUP WINNERS

FA Cup Leeds 1 Arsenal 0.
Football League Cup Chelsea 1 Stoke C 2
Scottish FA Cup Celtic 6 Hibernian 1
Scottish League Cup Celtic 1 Hibernian 2

NETZERED

German midfield master leaves England 3-1 down

IT WOULD be 1966 all over again, they said. Only thing is, can we close them down in Berlin and get the draw?

That, in a nutshell, was the national frame of mind as England prepared to meet West Germany at Wembley in the first leg of the quarter-finals of the European Championship (the former Nations Cup).

But if such breezy calculations had taken into account the known destructive power of Gerd Muller, and the calm generalship of Franz Beckenbauer, they

had certainly missed the critical factor. His name was Gunther Netzer, a flowing midfield genius who hadn't been around either in 1966 at Wembley or in 1970 at Leon.

When he got to Wembley, though, he tore up the England midfield, where there wasn't a ball-winner to stop him. The whole German side was electrified and won 3-1.

The return in Berlin was by comparison a dim 0-0 affair. But England had already been comprehensively eliminated on the night Netzer came to town.

TRANSFER MARKET

THE BRITISH record fee received a modest £5,000 increase when League Champions Derby acquired David Nish for £225,000 from Leicester. The record for a Third Division player was also broken when Manchester United acknowledged Ted MacDougall's run of 96 goals in two seasons for Bournemouth by paying out £200,000 for him.

That other Manchester club, City, also decided to splash £200,000 on Rodney Marsh from QPR. Meanwhile; for £30,000, Leeds made a shrewd investment in bringing Gordon McQueen south from St Mirren. Alistair Brown moved across the Midlands from Leicester to WBA for £55,000 and goalkeeper George Wood joined Blackpool from East Stirling for £7,000.

AS IN 1971 there were two British successes in the three European club tournaments, but the big one remained elusive. In fact it looks like becoming part of the furniture in the boardroom of Ajax. This year the Dutch champions retained the European Cup, beating a sadly unadventurous Inter-Milan.

More gratifying for home fans was the 3-2 victory in Barcelona which

sent the Cup Winners' Cup north to Glasgow. Rangers' Final opponents were Dynamo Moscow.

By the time of the Final of the UEFA Cup (old Fairs Cup), the foreign opposition had all been dealt with. Tottenham and Wolves won the right to fight it out among themselves. The Londoners with Alan Mullery back as captain after a spell on loan to Fulham, won 3-2 on aggregate.

IN THE GOALS

TED MACDOUGALL again finished well clear of the field with 47 goals for Third Division Bournemouth. Best in the other divisions were Francis Lee, with 33 League goals for Manchester City; Bob Latchford, 23 for Birmingham, and Matt Tees, 27 for Grimsby.

At the time Gordon Banks was, without argument, the greatest goalkeeper in the world. His save from Pele two years earlier during the Mexico World Cup had been photographed and analysed from every angle. And most people agreed with Pele that it was 'impossible and beyond belief'.

Now on a wet, cold night at West Ham, Banks was to equal that save. West Ham were one kick away from victory over Stoke City in a semi-final of the 1972 Football League Cup. One kick away from the Final at Wembley.

It was a penalty for West Ham. Geoff Hurst against Gordon Banks. Two revered England players; two friends. Hurst thrashed the ball towards the top right-hand corner of the net. His power and accuracy had rarely let him down. But now Banks soared towards the ball, met it firmly and had strength enough to turn it away for a corner. It was a save that silenced East London and set West Ham and Stoke down a road of replays that for raw-boned excitement have not been equalled in the history of the League Cup.

When the two clubs were drawn together for this semi-final there was already a special air about their meetings. West Ham were renowned for pure football and a fateful ability to throw away the juiciest gifts; Stoke were a happy, friendly club who for all their entertaining football over the years had never won a major trophy.

The semi-finals were over two legs and the first was at Stoke's Victoria Ground. There was nothing particularly memorable about it, but from this quiet, solid base a drama was to emerge.

West Ham won comfortably enough by 2-1 and might have won by more, according to their manager, Ron Greenwood. West Ham had started as favourites and deserved to, having already beaten Leeds, Liverpool and Sheffield United on the way.

Stoke's manager Tony Waddington went to the Post House Hotel outside Stoke after the game for a drink with Ron Greenwood. 'Tony was in the depths of despair,' Greenwood later recalled. 'He felt that Stoke had wasted a wonderful chance to win their first Cup in style.' With the second leg to come at West Ham it was easy to understand Waddington's disappointment.

Yet it was Stoke who had scored first at the Victoria Ground when Peter Dobing, a player with such a soft touch that you could be excused for thinking he played in carpet slippers, pushed the ball past Bobby Ferguson. Then Geoff Hurst put West Ham level with a penalty - smacked hard in his customary fashion, and even though Banks got a fingertip to the ball there was no stopping it.

'Gordon knows exactly where I put them,' Hurst said afterwards, 'but if you connect properly no goalkeeper on earth should be able to save them - not even Banksie.' These words were to haunt him exactly one week later.

Clyde Best rifled in a magnificent winning goal and West Ham celebrated as though the battle was over. Waddington also has memories of his visit to the Post House after the game. 'With Ron toasting his win and me drowning my sorrows we had a good night. But I wasn't totally downhearted. My experience with West Ham was that they were always likely to give you a chance to get back into the game. After all, twice in the League at Upton Park we had come back from being three goals down.'

Stoke did indeed play with much more fire and conviction in the second leg at Upton Park. It was a squelching night under the lights, the ball zipping off the turf. I remember commentating

on the match for ITV, determined not to let a natural London bias shine through, and there was much to praise Stoke for in a real red-blooded tie. Alan Bloor, that big bluff man who was so under-rated, Jack Marsh, the pugnacious Mike Pejic, Mike Bernard and, behind them, Gordon Banks were a battle-hardened defence that offered West Ham nothing. As Waddington had hoped, West Ham had their moment of charity. White-shirted Stoke launched another of their counter-attacks and John Ritchie, left unattended at the far post, scored. The

West Ham goalkeeper Bobby Ferguson, a pivotal figure in the saga, punches clear at Stoke in the opening game.

goal stunned a 38,000 West Ham crowd who were already counting the minutes that separated them from getting out their Wembley finery.

The game went into extra-time – and then came that memorable penalty. There were but a few seconds left when West Ham were through for what looked a certain equalizer. After a goalmouth skirmish in which Banks might once have been impeded as he tried to fall on the ball, the goalkeeper made a desperate rugby tackle on Harry Redknapp as he was about to slide the ball home.

Stoke's frantic mouthings over the foul on Banks were stonily disre-garded and the referee's finger pointed

John Ritchie's goal that won the second leg for Stoke 1–0. Ritchie had managed to get away from the attentions of Tommy Taylor, his marker, and when the long cross came over from the right the only man between Ritchie and **Ferguson, as the Stoke striker chested down the ball, was John McDowell. But McDowell had only taken up a general cover position and could not turn in time to prevent Ritchie from shooting home.**

to the spot. Four West Ham players were on their haunches facing their own goal. They dared not watch. What they missed was one of football's greatest saves as Banks hurled himself to connect with Hurst's thundering shot.

As Bobby Moore said afterwards: 'That was not a penalty *miss*-that was a penalty *save*.' And what did Banks do next? Like a truly great professional he angrily shrugged off the swarming congratulations of his teammates and harshly reminded them that there was still a corner to be faced. The corner was cleared, the final whistle was sounded and this amazing cup-tie circus next moved off to Hillsborough, home of Sheffield Wednesday.

The tie was, it seemed, slipping away from West Ham. But, inseparable from their obvious disappointment were questions that would not go away. Should Hurst have changed his method of taking penalties when it was obvious that Banks was well able to make a calculated guess which way the ball would go? Indeed, should Hurst have taken the kick at all?

Even to this day Ron Greenwood, now England's manager, still has it on his mind. 'Maybe I should have got somebody else to take it, or maybe Geoff should have slotted it into the other side of goal.' That agonizing choice was not lost on Hurst himself. He now says that he had thought of changing sides but was influenced by his success the previous week and his unswerving belief that if you hit them right nobody could touch them.

'I hit it well enough and there were no recriminations from my West Ham mates because they knew that was true,' said Hurst recently. 'Had I missed

Gordon Banks makes his super-save from Geoff Hurst's penalty.

badly, one or two were sure to have yelled at me, but they could see that it was a truly magnificent penalty save.'

'As to the fact that Ron felt someone else might have taken it, I believe no one else *could* have taken it. As it was, half of them couldn't find the nerve to watch.

'It was my worst moment in football – along with England's defeat in Leon in the 1970 World Cup. I had terrible nightmares about it that night and indeed for many weeks afterwards. That miss cost us a place at Wembley. And it was a miss that really changed my career. Had West Ham won I would have stayed with the club. As it was they decided to change things and I moved on, of all places, to Stoke.'

Before the replay at Hillsborough, there was trouble for West Ham even before they got to the ground. The team had finished off their preparations in Derbyshire's Peak District at Buxton. They misjudged the time it would take to get to the stadium and while they were still miles from it were desperately tangled up in traffic.

'You'll never get to the ground in time, you might as well turn back,' shouted an unsuspecting Yorkshire policeman. 'If we don't get to the ground there won't be a game,' was Greenwood's reply. And he ordered the driver, who had been late getting to Buxton in the first place, to drive down the wrong side of the road.

The trouble was, there was too little room for such a manoeuvre and the West Ham coach scraped six cars. So now the team coach was pursued by six cars with six angry drivers with insurance claims firmly on their minds.

Insurance claims were not on Greenwood's mind. He was worried that his team could become tense and ill-prepared for the match ahead. In fact

Trevor Brooking remembers that the team thought it was all a hilarious business and were not disturbed by it.

West Ham duly arrived at the ground 35 minutes before the kick-off only to find that Stoke had had similar problems on their drive in from Matlock. The heavy traffic reflected the growing interest in the series, and 46,000 fans at neutral Sheffield saw another exhilarating game that, in the time-honoured phrase, 'had everything but goals'. More superlative goalkeeping by Banks was matched this time by West Ham's Ferguson, and with Bobby Moore in command throughout the sides finished equal, which at least made sure that West Ham would have another chance.

Ron Greenwood lost the toss after the match to decide the next venue, and the second replay went to Old Trafford. 'After all our problems tonight on the way here, I knew I would lose the toss,' Greenwood groaned. But West Ham's night was not over yet. Somebody – maybe one of those battered-car drivers – had put sand in the petrol tank of the West Ham coach and the party was marooned at a deserted Hillsborough until a replacement could be found.

The game at Old Trafford gave this cup-tie its final and memorable flourish. It had started at Stoke on 15 December, and now it was to end on 26 January; 49,000 were there to see it, bringing the overall crowd total to 171,000.

It was another rainy night with the lights reflected back from the glistening mud in both goalmouths. Somehow you sensed it was a night for great deeds; a night when surely this marvel-

West Ham's defence under pressure in Match 3 – the replay thriller that 'had everything but goals'.

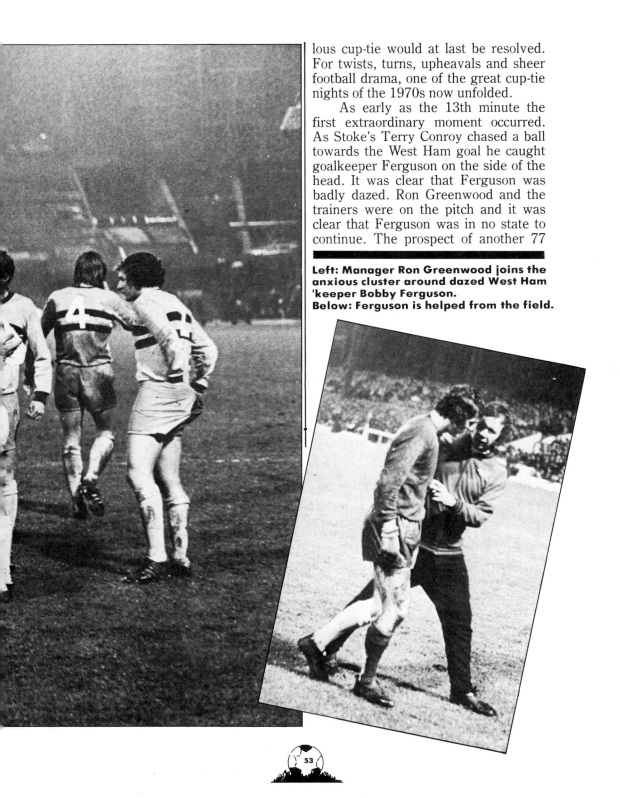

lous cup-tie would at last be resolved. For twists, turns, upheavals and sheer football drama, one of the great cup-tie nights of the 1970s now unfolded.

As early as the 13th minute the first extraordinary moment occurred. As Stoke's Terry Conroy chased a ball towards the West Ham goal he caught goalkeeper Ferguson on the side of the head. It was clear that Ferguson was badly dazed. Ron Greenwood and the trainers were on the pitch and it was clear that Ferguson was in no state to continue. The prospect of another 77

Left: Manager Ron Greenwood joins the anxious cluster around dazed West Ham 'keeper Bobby Ferguson.
Below: Ferguson is helped from the field.

53

minutes of a cup-tie without a 'keeper now faced West Ham as Ferguson stumbled to his feet, fell shakily to the ground once more and finally was helped away.

What confusion he left behind! Clyde Best was the nominated reserve goalkeeper but, on the night, the task was greater than his nerve. Ron Greenwood looked around for a likely volunteer in those tense moments as referee and crowd began to shout for more action.

It was Bobby Moore who got the nod. The man with the refrigerator mind and a vast store of big-time experience now took over the green jersey. It was a gamble to take his calming talents from the middle of the defence, but it was one that West Ham had to take. Twice before, the England captain had taken over between the posts: once in a reserve match against Crystal Palace and once in the League against Chelsea, and he had not conceded a goal.

In the mud and rain at Old Trafford that night, Moore was still close enough to his peak as a footballer to give an air of confidence and competence as he went about his work. West Ham protected him well and his catching and stopping were never less than comfortable.

But it could not last. West Ham, having been awarded two penalties in earlier games, now had one given against them. Full-back John McDowell, pursued by panic, had recklessly conceded it while trying to compensate for a fatally weak back-pass.

Stoke defender Mike Bernard took the kick, and for one incredible moment it seemed that Moore had saved it as he dived to his right to parry the ball. Sadly for West Ham's hopes the ball rebounded into the path of the relieved Bernard, who slipped it into the other side of the net.

Moore later said: 'It must have got to Mike Bernard that he ought to beat someone like me who wasn't a proper goalkeeper. I took a guess and dived to my right and the ball came that way and I went to push it around the post. But it was such a bad penalty that it was closer to me than I expected, and I was all tucked up when I made the save. The goalmouth seemed the loneliest place in the world. I felt like a prisoner caged in by the edge of the penalty box.'

'A pity you couldn't catch it,' said Greenwood jokingly in the dressing-room at half-time. By then West Ham were getting back into the mood for jokes. Since the penalty their 10 men – playing with the spirit of 20 – had astonished everyone by going into a 2-1 lead. Buccaneering runs through the midfield by Billy Bonds had begun to lift West Ham hearts, and it was fitting that he should have scored West Ham's equalizing goal, hitting a strong shot that was deflected wide of Banks. Soon after, Trevor Brooking helped to create a clever goal which he scored himself. Who now could tell what else the night might hold?

During this time Mr Greenwood and Ferguson had not been idle. The manager had been throwing balls to his stricken goalkeeper in the tunnel as he looked for something in Ferguson's eyes to suggest that he knew what he was about. Ferguson was still slightly concussed, but the verdict was: 'Get out there, stand between the posts, do your

A thoughtful Bobby Moore pulls on the green jersey as he takes his place between the posts. Could the England captain, unbeaten in his two previous spells as a stand-in goalkeeper for West Ham, in lesser matches against Crystal Palace and Chelsea, shut out a Stoke side now so hungry for success?

best and we'll do our best to protect you.'

So, in numbers at least, West Ham were back to full-strength. But the protective ring around Ferguson could not stop Dobing from stealing in for a Stoke equalizer early in the second half.

The pendulum now swung once more towards Stoke as they began to hit long-range shots towards the dazed Ferguson. Some were cut out, some went sailing too high, and some were bundled away by the 'keeper until Terry Conroy at last struck a shot from far beyond the penalty area that Ferguson could only acknowledge as it soared

past him on its way into the net.

West Ham rallied, but those first-half efforts when they were down to 10 men had left them with nothing in reserve. Hurst felt he might have had another penalty when he was brought down, but an advantage was played and then it was over.

Above left to below right: Four steps to misery for Moore and his Hammers. Mike Bernard hits a weak penalty which Moore correctly reads and gets to but can only push back into the path of the grateful Stoke man who then rams the ball home past Moore's left side.

STOKE CITY F.C.

Wednesday March 22nd 1972
Kick-off 7.30 pm
F.A. CUP ROUND 6 Replay

STOKE CITY
v
MANCHESTER UNITED

OFFICIAL
PROGRAMME

6p

Ferguson said afterwards that he couldn't remember anything about the game. Over the years, many have been more than prepared to tell him of one of football's greatest nights.

His opposite number, who had so kept alive Stoke's hopes, was determined to enjoy the memory of the triumph. At the final whistle Tony Waddington's eyes switched straight to his goalkeeper. 'At the end Gordon was on his knees, looking up to the sky, praying his

thanks to someone up there. It was a marvellous moment, happily captured by a photographer, and I used the picture on the front of our programme for months. But he was just one of a team who never knew when they were

Below: Match programmes for the Hillsborough and Old Trafford replays.
Opposite: Gordon Banks thanks God it's over. This image stirred Stoke manager Tony Waddington enough to use it on the front of the club's programme.

done for. We battled and battled so much that we felt we could go on indefinitely.'

Ron Greenwood, looking back, believes West Ham were never meant to win. 'The fates decided that Stoke would take the tie from the very first,' he says. 'We should have sewn up the very first game, we missed that vital penalty in the second, and then losing our goalkeeper in the last game was just too much.'

Stoke went on to the Final at Wembley where they beat Chelsea 2-1 and so won their first major trophy since they were formed in 1863. They were popular winners too, with still a touch of the fairy-story about their victory. George Eastham, the creative midfield player, epitomized Tony Waddington's flair for eking everything from ageing talents, and it was he who scored the winner.

**Opposite: Bubbly for Terry Conroy.
Below: Cheering Stoke fans, their dreams of League Cup glory answered by the promise of a trip to Wembley.**

LEAGUE UPS AND DOWNS

Division I
Champions Liverpool, runners-up Arsenal. Relegated Crystal Palace, WBA.

Division II
Champions Burnley, also promoted QPR. Relegated Huddersfield T, Brighton.

Division III
Champions Bolton W, also promoted Notts Co. Relegated Rotherham U, Brentford, Swansea C, Scunthorpe U.

Division IV
Champions Southport, also promoted Hereford U, Cambridge U, Aldershot.

Scottish Division I
Champions Celtic, runners-up Rangers. Relegated Kilmarnock, Airdrie.

Division II
Champions Clyde, also promoted Dunfermline A.

Europe...

AJAX OF Amsterdam laid claims to being a team in the mould of the great Real Madrid sides of the 1950s when they carried off the European Cup, beating Juventus 1-0 in Belgrade.

British hopes were pinned on Derby County until they went down 3-1 to Juventus in the first leg of the semi-final and could only draw 0-0 in the home fixture.

Leeds once more faltered at the last jump when they lost 1-0 to AC Milan in the Final of the Cup Winners' Cup.

In the UEFA Cup Final, on-form Liverpool, the new Division I champions, took on Borussia Mönchengladbach. They had the confidence and skill to knock in three goals at Anfield and then scraped home by losing 0-2 in the away leg.

TRANSFER MARKET

BRITISH PRICES were dwarfed by the awesome £900,000 that changed hands when Johan Cruyff travelled south from Ajax to join Barcelona.

Gary Sprake fetched a goalkeeper's record of £100,000 in his move from Leeds to Birmingham. And Ted Macdougall still commanded a respectable £145,000 when he was bought by Norwich from West Ham.

Stewart Houston, formerly with Chelsea, looked set once more for higher things, leaving Brentford for Manchester United at a fee of £55,000.

Unhappy Graeme Souness moved more than halfway home to Scotland by joining Middlesbrough from Spurs for £30,000. While a little-known striker, Derek Hales, was transferred from Luton to Charlton for £10,000.

Magnificent Sunderland..

A FIERCE volley from Ian Porterfield's 'wrong' right foot in the 31st minute was enough to make Sunderland the first Second Division side to lift the FA Cup since WBA in 1931. Leeds responded furiously after Porterfield's goal, but the Wearsiders' 'keeper Jim Montgomery surpassed himself with some wonderful saves. He was supported by superb defence work, with Dave Watson outstanding, and the kind of luck that long-odds outsiders must have if they are to survive at Wembley.

The true turning-point came after 65 minutes. Sunderland had snatched their surprise lead after half an hour, but then Reaney crossed from the right and Cherry ran in to thump a firm header towards the far corner.

Somehow Montgomery got to the ball and beat it down, but only into the path of Peter Lorimer. The Leeds man hit the rebound powerfully. The ball flew towards the net, only for Montgomery to twist across the face of the goal and touch it on to the underside of his bar. The ball was hooked away and Bob Stokoe's boys must have known then that they were in with a real chance.

Towards the end Sunderland were even stretching Harvey in the Leeds goal. Horswill galloped everywhere, Halom went close, and after 90 minutes a newcomer would have been hard-pressed to say which side was to finish 3rd in the Football League and which 28th!

At the final whistle, Sunderland manager Bob Stokoe raced onto the pitch to embrace Jim Montgomery and the Sunderland skipper Bobby Kerr rushed to the bench to replace the gap in his grin with gleaming white teeth . . . and proudly led his team up to the Royal Box.

NEWS IN BRIEF

■ Celtic's League championship made a record eight in a row.
■ Ted Croker took over as FA Secretary.
■ In the power crisis at the end of the year, the Government ruled that all matches must take place in daylight. Floodlights were banned even where generators were available.

HOME CUP WINNERS	
FA Cup Sunderland 1 Leeds U 0	1 Norwich C 0
Football League Cup Tottenham H	**Scottish FA Cup** Rangers 3 Celtic 2
	Scottish League Cup Celtic 1 Hibernian 2

IN THE GOALS

WOLVES' JOHN Richards was the season's top striker with 33 League and Cup goals. His nearest Division I rival was 'Pop' Robson, with 28 for West Ham. In the lower reaches, Arthur Horsfield scored 29 for Charlton and Fred Binney netted the same number for Exeter C.

October 17, 1973. Arguably the most significant football date in the '70s. Certainly the most frustrating and bitterly disappointing. The night England could only draw 1-1 at Wembley with Poland, thus failing to qualify for the World Cup finals, an absence from the game's top occasion that was to span the rest of the decade.

There are still those who contest that the qualifying place was really lost before that night, when earlier in the year a point in the qualifying group was dropped at home to Wales and two fell by the wayside in a cacophonous atmosphere in Chorzow. Nevertheless England's task at Wembley remained straightforward. A win over Poland would be enough.

Encouragingly, three weeks earlier England had overrun Austria 7-0, the thrashing Sir Alf Ramsey had always been promising his England team would deliver once the finishing matched the thorough approach. The victory had been achieved without Bobby Moore, who had been dropped by West Ham and was therefore ruled out of the international by lack of top-class match practice, and Alan Ball, sent off in Chorzow, and banned from the next World Cup game. Instead, England were led by Martin Peters, with that perennial understudy, Norman Hunter, taking Moore's role as a player, while the buoyant Tony Currie had been given a place in midfield. The entire nation had waited for Ramsey to decide on whether to play Moore. The success against Austria prevented a recall, but England's manager had not forgotten his qualities. 'I expect to qualify for the finals,' he told Moore, 'and I'll need you to captain the squad in Munich.'

Television had been understandably quick to appreciate the drama of the visit of Poland and the sudden-death quality of the contest. ITV, in the scheme of alternation with the BBC, had the rights to cover the match, and with the game a guaranteed sell-out an extra outlay bought live coverage. It was also the time when Brian Clough, then manager of Derby County, was a regular contributor to ITV's football programmes.

It was with Brian and Peter Taylor, in fact, that my involvement with the Poles began. The week prior to their trip to England they warmed-up in Rotterdam against Holland and the three of us travelled with a film unit to file a preview story for 'On the Ball'. On first sight at training, I was struck by the apparent nervousness of the Polish players. Pale and unsure of themselves, they looked like men who were on their way to the gallows. And yet maybe that is where the first clue should have been spotted that they were going to present a problem. They had come out of Poland, after all, almost a fortnight before their Wembley fixture – precious time to forge a uniting team spirit.

As Olympic champions, too, Poland were not without pedigree. Yet though they managed to draw 1-1 with Holland – Kazimierz Deyna scoring an impressive goal – the class came from the Dutch. Certainly Brian Clough and Peter Taylor were not alone in feeling that England would face an uncomplicated task. The subsequent interview with Brian for 'On the Ball' was to give the Poles – or rather a key member of their team – a label that remains to this day. It was Clough's view – substantiated by Peter, a former goalkeeper himself – that Jan Tomaszewski in Poland's goal was a 'clown'. Taylor was even moved by Poland's timidity in Rotterdam to call them a team of 'donkeys'.

Tomaszewski, big, awkward and palpably inexperienced, had certainly injected uncertainty into Poland's defence in Holland. How much more would he do so amid the tension of Wembley? Surely it could only work to England's advantage. The ITV entourage returned to London in a mood of great optimism. And it was a trip which was to have great personal ramifications for the two experts.

On Monday 15 October, Brian Clough and Peter Taylor resigned from Derby County in response to a letter from Sam Longson, the club chairman, asking for them to discontinue their work for television. The story rivalled that of the forthcoming international itself for media space, and the next day Brian was on the panel of ITV's 'Who Will Win the International?' preview programme. On match night he took his place on the panel of experts along with Malcolm Allison and Jack Charlton. Since those days Brian has certainly mellowed, but a reminder of his abrasiveness was the feeling prevalent at that time that fifty per cent loved him, fifty per cent hated him, but everybody watched him.

One aspect of the match that concerned our panel was the possibility of violence. The same night that England had been sharpening their teeth against Austria, Poland had played Wales in Chorzow in the World Cup qualifers. It had been a match far removed not only from the rules of football, but the Queensberry Rules as well. Trevor Hockey had been sent off, and certainly Wales had been no injured innocents. But with memory of the Alan Ball incident in Chorzow still fresh, there was the fear that though the Poles were expected to go down, they might well go down fighting. The presence of Belgian referee Vital Loreaux, though, was reassuring; at 48, too old according to Football League regulations, his vast experience made him a sound choice.

In terms of team selection Sir Alf Ramsey sprang no surprises. Loyalty had always been uppermost in his priorities and now he was loyal to those who had swept Austria aside. Leicester City's Peter Shilton in goal. Paul Madeley and Emlyn Hughes at full-back, with a central pairing of Roy McFarland and Norman Hunter, and Bobby Moore left to sit on the bench. Colin Bell, Martin Peters and Tony Currie in midfield. And a three-pronged attack of Martin Chivers, Allan Clarke and Mick Channon. Ramsey had admitted that it had been a mistake not to include Channon from the start in Chorzow.

For the record, Poland's line-up read: Tomaszewski, Szymanowski, Gorgon, Musial, Bulzacki, Kasperczak, Lato, Cmikiewicz, Deyna, Domarski, Gadocha. Several names still have a meaning in a world context at the end of the decade, but they were names that meant little to the watching millions on the night of 17 October 1973. Surely they were cast as bit-part performers on a night when England would hold the centre of the stage.

For once, that certain reserve that had not numbered Wembley crowds amongst the world's most passionate was totally absent. The days of Don Revie's Land of Hope and Glory were still to come, but the importance of the occasion had shed the inhibitions. Still to come, too, were the days of international kit emblazoned with manufacturers' insignia. England wore traditional plain white with dark blue shorts. Poland played in all red. After Martin Peters, on the night the only survivor from England's 1966 World Cup win, had tossed up with Kazimierz Deyna, England attacked the tunnel end. Or should I say Tomaszewski defended it!

Headquarters:

HOMESTEAD COURT HOTEL
WELWYN GARDEN CITY, HERTFORDSHIRE
(Telephone No.: 96-24336)

**ARRANGEMENTS FOR TRAVEL
AND ACCOMMODATION**

SUNDAY, 14th OCTOBER, 1973

ASSEMBLY. All players should make their own travelling arrangements in order to arrive at Whites Hotel, Lancaster Gate, London, W.2. (Telephone No: 01-262 2711) by 18.00 hours.

18.00 hours   Depart from Whites Hotel by motor coach for the Homestead Court Hotel, Welwyn Garden City, Herts.

MONDAY, 15th OCTOBER, 1973

Detailed arrangements for the day will be announced at Headquarters.

TUESDAY, 16th OCTOBER, 1973

10.30 hours   Training session at the B.A.C. Sports Ground, Bragbury End, Stevenage.
13.00 hours   Lunch at Headquarters.
Arrangements for the afternoon and evening will be announced at Headquarters.

WEDNESDAY, 17th OCTOBER, 1973

10.30 hours   Training session at the B.A.C. Sports Ground, Bragbury End, Stevenage.
13.00 hours   Lunch at Headquarters.
17.45 hours   Depart from Homestead Court Hotel by motor coach with police escort for Wembley Stadium.

19.45 hours   ENGLAND v. POLAND

Players will be free to disperse after the match but hotel accommodation will be available in London for any players who may require it for Wednesday night.

**Opposite: Programmes for the two England-Poland matches, played at Chorzow and Wembley.
Left: FA instructions to the England players outline the three-day build-up to the Wembley decider.**

Even now experts disagree as to whether Tomaszewski had been wrongly daubed in a clown's make-up by Brian Clough – whether really this tall gangling, open-faced goalkeeper was really far better than we had been led to believe. Controversy was never to leave him through his career, and yet he was to grace two World Cups, one with enormous distinction. Certainly, though, he defied England with a display of brilliant goal-keeping during which luck and some heroic defenders were never too distant from his side.

England, at times nervously, at times fluently, chipped away in the first half during which they ran up a catalogue of nail-biting misses that remain in the ITV archives as an ever-frustrating testimony to what might have been. Here are just five of them.

Martin Peters chipped a free-kick to the far post. McFarland stretched to turn the ball across the face of the goal where from close range Channon bundled it against Tomaszewski's right-hand post.

Channon twisted to meet a driven cross by Currie but his firm header dropped over the bar.

Tomaszewski showed his first flash of brilliance, plunging low to his right to turn aside a fierce right-footed drive from Colin Bell.

Tomaszewski now flung himself to his left to reach a subtle deflected header from Clarke that was perfectly placed just inside the upright.

Another Channon header was dipping under the bar, before the giant Polish goalkeeper stretched back to finger-tip it to safety.

At half-time Brian Clough's comments, like his others about Tomaszewski, were to earn him the castigation of the nation. And yet his theme seemed so right at the time. He told all the viewers at home to relax, that it would all come good for England. In its way it was a brilliant piece of television because it was what everyone wanted to hear, and it was justified because England were so in command. Poland had barely threatened, but in fact it was Malcolm Allison who threw in a word of warning that in hindsight had a chilling accuracy. Despite England's pressure Big Mal had an uneasy feeling that England were vulnerable to a sucker punch.

That prophecy was fulfilled in a moment that in effect ended England's World Cup hopes. Norman Hunter found himself dragged over to the touchline

Tomaszewski makes a superb save, turning away Bell's fierce drive. Currie, on the left, has one arm raised in readiness, but the first half was barren of goals.

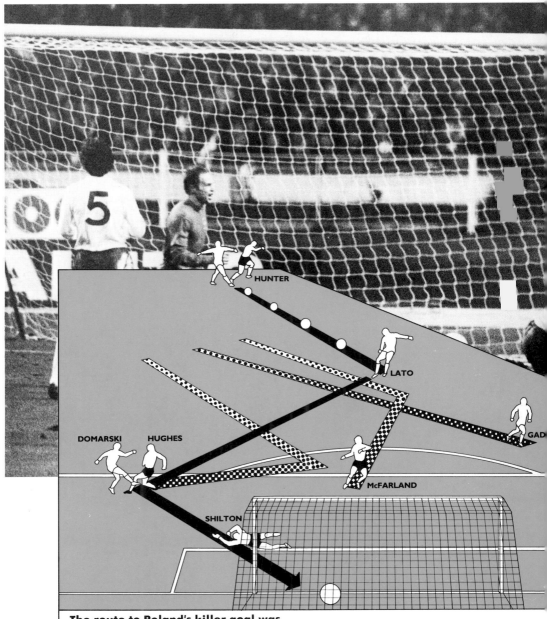

The route to Poland's killer goal was founded by Lato's run past Hunter on the Polish left. Lato drew the English defence and slipped the ball to Domarski whose shot deceived Shilton and passed under the 'keeper's body.

right in front of the Royal Box, Poland's left and England's right. The most fearsome tackler in England, however, contrived to miss out on his attempt to stop Lato, and the Pole sped clear. Drawing the cover towards him Lato intelligently played the ball off to his right where Domarski arrived to shoot beneath the dive of the underworked Shilton.

Only years of brilliant consistency wiped the question mark of the goal from Shilton's record. He recalls: 'Along with my error in the European Cup semi-final against Cologne it was one of my most important mistakes. But against Poland it honestly was not quite as bad as it looked. The shot from Domarski came through Emlyn Hughes's legs as he stretched across him to block the effort. The ball arrived too close for me to make a real dive at and yet not close enough to block with my body. It's only some excuse but I don't believe it was quite as bad as people thought at the time. And after all we missed plenty at the other end.'

To England's credit they took

Shilton on his knees after the tragedy that for years destroyed his international credibility.

only six minutes to recover from the numbing shock, beating Tomaszewski at last with a coolly executed Allan Clarke penalty. But the 'clown' was not to be beaten again, even though England laid siege to his goal.

First Chivers, breaking through the centre, laid off a shooting chance for Currie. On his left foot, the Sheffield United man sliced the ball desperately wide.

From 25 yards, Currie found the

target, but Tomaszewski matched power with power to fist out the shot. The ball flew straight to Channon whose lightning reaction was to volley it back towards the unattended goal. From a tight angle the shot arrowed into the side-netting.

The Flying Pole, whose acrobatics, skill and good fortune took Poland to the 1974 finals in West Germany.

Currie, again, now crossing from the right, watched in disbelief as the ball eluded Tomaszewski to roll along the top of the crossbar.

Tomaszewski, caught in no man's land, out by the penalty spot and stumbling to the ground, somehow kicked away Clarke's effort to drive the ball past him.

Hunter, thrown forward by Ramsey to stretch Poland down England's left, cut in on his right foot. Tomaszewski again chose to beat away the shot rather than catch it and the ball fell kindly for the Poles.

Clarke, leaning back, headed just over from a deep right-wing cross.

Currie yet again produced a shot from outside the penalty area which lanced past the red-shirted defenders but not past Tomaszewski.

Hughes's rampaging run down the left ended in a cross that Bell would surely have reached right in front of goal had he not been thumped to the ground. Before the penalty appeals had been formed on the lips the ball dropped for Clarke who, from close in, again found Tomaszewski unbeatable. The referee, figuring England had been given the advantage, refused subsequent claims for a spot-kick.

Inside the last 90 seconds Kevin Hector's fateful header was scrambled off the line as far as Clarke who, caught horribly off-balance, could only stab at the ball and direct it wide.

Though Hector's effort is always remembered as the final moment of despair there was still time for Bell's low thrust to beat Tomaszewski only for Gorgon to fling himself along the line in Poland's ultimate act of rescue.

At the final whistle Bobby Moore was first across to console an agonized Hunter in a picture that will remain in my mind for a long time. Sir Alf Ramsey, outwardly as stoical as ever, faced our television cameras within ten minutes of the final whistle, while the reporters from Polish television waited their turn to send vastly different tidings to their country. In fact their report set out to be a straight interview with Gorski, the manager, but one by one the players, normally so reticent as players are from Eastern Europe, simply joined in unannounced. On another night it would have been hilarious to watch.

I was left with half an hour to do on live television which we had planned in anticipation of jubilant comment and the need to look forward to England's chances in West Germany. It was an extremely difficult experience with everyone flat on their backs, like doing a half-hour commentary on a funeral. Brian Clough, in character I suppose, still had time for one further surprise. Even though he had been a regular, outspoken critic of Ramsey he now spoke out in his defence, and once we were off the air he went straight down to the dressing-rooms to commiserate with Sir Alf. 'We are both football managers and I know how he must be feeling now,' he explained.

As far as the public was concerned, both men were to be blamed. Ramsey's own stature had been deeply harmed by failing to live up to the standards he set for himself with the 1966 World Cup win. This defeat effectively finished him, though it was not until the following May that his appointment was terminated. His lack of ease in introducing substitutes had been roundly criticized three years earlier in Leon. Now the introduction of Hector, only two minutes from time and then only at the insistence of Bobby Moore, was ridiculed.

After the match, Norman Hunter does not seek to conceal his agony. On reflection, few were to complain that his error alone cost England the match.

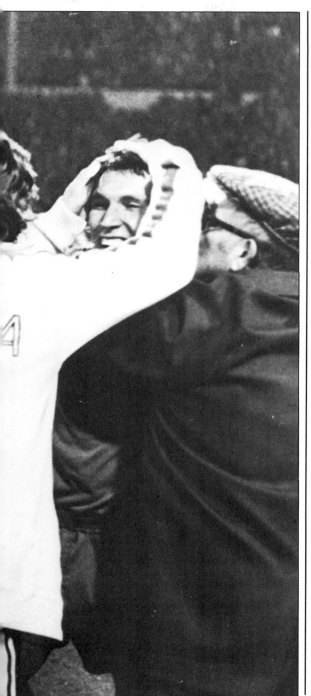

Tomaszewski's performance had flown in the face of Brian Clough's comments, though it is interesting to recall quotes from the following day's *Daily Mirror*. Ray Clemence thought he had made some diabolical mistakes and got away with them. Pat Jennings said that he had never seen 'a bloke play so badly and so great inside one match'.

The England players too had their careers affected by the result. Martin Chivers, a slumbering giant on the night, walked out of international football at the moment Hector raced into it for that last dreadfully belated gamble. Hector himself was to savour only one further England cap, again as a substitute. Hunter, whose family were wickedly abused for his error, lost much of his international credibility at a time when he might have taken over totally from Moore. Currie was to win only two caps in the next four and a half years, while Shilton had to live with the voices of criticism. Scotland's qualification for the final stages just threw England's failure into sharper relief.

Some of the pain of defeat was reduced by the marvellous account that Poland gave of themselves in the World Cup finals. Their win over Italy in the first-round group not only eliminated one of the most fancied countries, but produced a truly memorable match. That they did not reach the World Cup Final itself was more a reflection on freak weather conditions in Frankfurt than their own shortcomings in what was to all intents a semi-final against West Germany. Tomaszewski saved a penalty from Hoeness (his second penalty save of the finals) only to be beaten by

By contrast with England's thunderstruck team, the Poles went in for wholesale celebration that later bubbled over into a jubilant contest to reach the micro-phone and speak to viewers back home.

Gerd Muller, who retained his balance in the morass of mud to score after Poland's attackers had lost their balance when faced by a number of similar openings.

Poland's final placing, third, did not flatter the quality in the side, which surely drew great self-belief from surviving the Wembley ordeal. Two years later they were to take the silver medal in the Montreal Olympics (after Tomaszewski had been substituted in the Final) and qualified subsequently for the 1978 World Cup finals. There a missed penalty by Deyna contributed not only to their own failure to go beyond the second round but to Argentina's eventual progression to winning the competition.

So, on reflection, the Pole-axing of England in 1973 said much about the spreading of standards in world football. Watching a re-run of those extraordinary misses only serves as a desperate reminder that in every aspect except putting the ball into the net, combined with one heavily punished defensive catastrophe, England played well. Yet the result condemned England to a spell in the international backwaters. The change that the failure provoked did not lead to any really significant international success for the rest of the decade.

As Kevin Hector, denied by inches from a place in the game's folk-lore, would surely echo, success in football hangs on a fine thread. And England's thread broke on the night of 17 October 1973.

Gorgon after the final whistle hugs teammate Cmikiewicz. English observers had been quick to tag the massive defender with adjectives such as 'lumbering', but it was his clearance off the line in the final seconds that denied England their all-important victory.

THE GAZETTE

IN THE GOALS

Top man in the Football League was Gillingham's Brian Yeo with a League and Cup haul of 32. Best in the other Divisions were: **Division I** Malcolm Macdonald (Newcastle U) 25 goals **Division II** Duncan McKenzie (Nottingham F) 28 goals **Division III** Billy Jennings (Watford) 29 goals

TRANSFER MARKET

MANY OF the year's big deals involved unsettled Chelsea. OUT went Alan Hudson, to Stoke for £240,000, followed by Peter Osgood who left for Southampton in exchange for £275,000. IN came David Hay, bought from Celtic for £225,000.

Greater sums changed hands when Bob Latchford moved from Birmingham to Everton. His fee -£350,000. Martin Dobson also joined Everton, leaving Burnley for a £300,000 fee, while Peter Shilton set a world record for a goalkeeper when Stoke paid Leicester £325,000 for him.

At Liverpool, Bill Shankly's last buy was Ray Kennedy from Arsenal for £200,000, while for his opening deal new manager Bob Paisley paid £60,000 to Northampton for Phil Neal.

Former England captain Bobby Moore went from West Ham to Fulham for a modest £25,000.

LEAGUE UPS AND DOWNS

Division I
Champions Leeds, runners-up Liverpool. Relegated Southampton, Manchester U, Norwich C.
Division II
Champions Middlesbrough (by 15 points!), also promoted Luton T, Carlisle U. Relegated Crystal Palace, Preston NE, Swindon T.
Division III
Champions Oldham A, also promoted Bristol R, York C. Relegated
Cambridge U, Shrewsbury T, Southport, Rochdale.
Division IV
Champions Peterborough U, also promoted Gillingham, Colchester U, Bury.
Scottish Division I
Champions Celtic, runners-up Hibernian. Relegated East Fife, Falkirk.
Division II
Champions Airdrieonians, also promoted Kilmarnock.

HOME CUP WINNERS

FA Cup
Liverpool 3
Newcastle U 0
Football League Cup Wolves 2
Manchester C 1

Scottish FA Cup
Celtic 3, Dundee U 0
Scottish League Cup Dundee 1, Celtic 0

MANAGERS EXCUSE ME

THE DEADLY combination of Old Father Tyme and poor results led to an extraordinary bout of managerial retirements and sackings in the upper reaches of the English game.

The sacking of Sir Alf came when, on 1 May, the FA announced that he was no longer England team manager. They made Joe Mercer his caretaker replacement. On 4 July the favourite contender, Don Revie, was appointed to the 'permanent' job. Revie's departure created an opening at Leeds. On 20 July Brian Clough left Brighton to take over at Elland Road. After 4 days he was sacked. His previous public criticism of the club and its players proved too big a hurdle even for Clough to clear.

An earlier dressing-room revolt had forced out Ron Saunders at Manchester City, but another at Stamford Bridge rebounded on Peter Osgood, who went while Chelsea manager Dave Sexton stayed - but only for seven months, then he was sacked. In October Sexton's departure from Chelsea began another chain reaction. Gordon Jago vacated the position at QPR and settled in at Millwall, while Sexton moved to QPR.

Oh dear Dino!

Dino Zoff's record of 12 successive shut-outs ends as Haiti take the lead in Munich.

If football is judged on its ability to excite, and on the combination of high-quality individual skills co-ordinated by sophisticated teamwork, the team of the decade took the world stage in 1974. Like Hungary 20 years earlier, Holland ended with no crown to show for their talents—both nations, coincidentally, bowing to West Germany. Yet the abiding memory of the 1974 World Cup is of the Dutch, who lifted soccer on to a higher plane.

In retrospect Holland's impact on the tournament should have come as no surprise. In 1970 Feyenoord of Rotterdam had ended Jock Stein's tilt at a second European Cup victory, and in the same competition the next three years belonged to Ajax of Amsterdam. Thirteen players from these two clubs were in Rinus Michels' squad of 22, plus Johan Cruyff who had recently left Ajax for new challenges with Barcelona.

'Total football' was the label pinned to the Dutch style, a tag that emphasized the free-wheeling approach in which attackers and defenders intermingled. With a high level of individual technique throughout their side, defenders like Haan and Krol were just as likely to arrive as the furthest player forward. Because of the awareness of the covering men, and the strong sense of team play, such freedom was rarely costly.

Even in defence Holland provided inventiveness, attacking the opponent in possession in groups in massed charges like some orange-shirted cavalry. Nor did their aesthetic qualities hide a soft centre. Prior to the 1978 World Cup finals Rudi Krol admitted misgivings about Brazil. 'I think they are a dirty side,' he declared, having seen five Brazilians booked at Wembley. When

that part of the interview was mentioned to Arie Haan, the Dutchman replied with a smile, 'Yes, but we can be dirty too!' They certainly never shirked the physical side of the game in 1974, and Brazil, more than any of Holland's opponents, would have cause to remember that.

British hopes to the World Cup finals revolved around Scotland. Where England had failed, Willie Ormond's side had qualified to join the 15 other nations in West Germany. On an ecstatic night at Hampden Park the previous September, Scotland had sealed their place by coming from behind to beat Czechoslovakia. While England were missing from the finals for the first time since before the war, Scotland had not qualified since Sweden in 1958.

It was a time when diehard English journalists, who privately regarded Scotland as traditionally their greatest enemy, wore a Scottish favour. ITV's World Cup panel were whisked off to the Scotch House in Knightsbridge to be kitted out in tartan jackets, and the preview shown on the eve of the competition was entitled 'Can Scotland Win?'

It was a time for prediction, and among the experts Holland were barely considered, only the panel's chairman plumping for an outright Dutch victory. Sir Alf Ramsey, Brian Clough, Jack Charlton and Pat Crerand selected, accurately as it turned out, a triumph for West Germany. Brazil were the choice of Derek Dougan and Malcolm Allison, while Bobby Moncur put his faith in Italy. Cruyff was on everyone's list of outstanding players to watch out for, but he was the only Dutchman.

Pre-finals gossip emanating from the Dutch camp did little to help their cause. There were disputes about money, and about whether the players' wives should be allowed in the headquarters.

Nine Ajax players had threatened to quit the squad and only the appointment of Rinus Michels as manager brought order. Yet Michels, who commanded respect among the players, only accepted the post on a short-term basis. Even before a ball was kicked in West Germany, the Dutch FA had seen fit to announce that George Knobel would succeed Michels, thereby creating further feelings of confusion.

There is a complexity in the Dutch character that has made the impact of their national side somewhat surprising. More than most nations, they have suffered a preference for club over country from their star players. Cruyff was not the only Dutchman to opt out of the 1978 finals. Ruud Geels, a prolific striker whose goal sense was greatly missed, and Jan van Beveren, the first-choice goalkeeper, opted to stay at home. Another mysterious absentee was Jan Peters (who in 1977 scored both goals in Holland's 2-0 win at Wembley); he dropped out with an injury discovered almost at the last minute. And right at the point of departure Wim van Hanegem, a classic influence in 1974, walked out on the squad when he was told he would not be a first choice in midfield.

The intelligence of the Dutch players, whose magnificent sense of public relations is heightened by their ability to answer questions with equal facility in a variety of European tongues, at times acts against the common good of the team as they continually question those who direct them. Nor are they the most optimistic of races. In Buenos Aires in 1978 Rudi Krol put their temperament into perspective: 'Here we are on the eve of our second successive World Cup Final, which is really a magnificent achievement. You English ask us about how we are going to play, but not the Dutch journalists. They all want to know how we are going to feel when we have lost!'

But in 1974 Holland were not the only country undergoing a less-than-happy preparation. The discipline in the Scotland camp was open to question when Jimmy Johnstone, Celtic's winger, was found drifting at sea in a rowing boat. When the team decamped from their base on the Ayrshire coast for preparation matches in Europe, both Johnstone and Billy Bremner, the captain, missed the team curfew and were threatened with being sent home, though neither was. The players also took issue with the agent appointed by the Scottish FA to negotiate their perks.

In the event Scotland performed creditably, though finally without success. Their great failure was not to punish the African outsiders Zaire by more than the two goals scored by the Leeds pair, Jordan and Lorimer. Their Group rivals, Yugoslavia, helped themselves to nine goals against Zaire's unsophisticated defence, while the three Brazil claimed were, in the final analysis, just enough to edge out the Scots.

Scotland's finest hour came in holding Brazil, the holders, to a goalless draw, in which Bremner rewarded the faith of his manager with a buccaneering display. Needing to beat Yugoslavia to

Emergent and established stars: Lato of Poland, above, and Cruyff, left, here leaping clear. Below: Finals programme cover.

advance in the competition, Ormond's side could fashion no more than another draw, and left for home after the first round–though they had conceded only one goal and not lost a match. Back in the ITV studios the tartan jackets were hung up for the last time, some to be given away as raffle prizes in a charity bazaar.

In their opening match Holland needed all their athleticism to dodge some ferocious tackling from Uruguay, who had Montero-Castillo sent off by the Hungarian referee Palotai. Rep avoided the challenges to open the scoring in the seventh minute, and he

ensured a win with a second goal four minutes from time. But rumours about Dutch discontent over their payments for the competition lingered on, particularly after they managed only a goalless draw against the part-timers from Sweden. Their insipid performance produced accusations of not-trying which caused bitter argument in the studio.

Brian Clough defended the Holland players: 'I think you do my profession an injustice by inferring that a couple of footballers went on to the field not wanting to play. I'll not sit here and infer that people will play and not give their absolute lot. They've had a lot of

stick for the commercial aspects. But they'll get none of that from me. It's not on.' But Bobby Moncur was not so sure: 'I watched the whole match and I can see when a player is not having a go. I'm not saying the whole team did it but one or two did.'

Certainly Sweden's subsequent performance in reaching the second round and giving West Germany a genuine test suggested that they were no pushover. Yet Holland were clearly out of sorts, just as they were to be four years later when a number of players freely admitted they would be happy not to qualify for the second round after

Opposite: Opening skirmishes. Bremner goes forward for Scotland against Zaire, above, and Swedish dangerman Sandberg (11) is closely watched by West Germany's Vogts. Above: Holland at the start of the tournament.

a similar goalless draw in their second match, against Peru. The Dutch certainly produce complex athletes!

Then in Dortmund on 23 June, Holland recovered their appetite. The first of two first-half penalties thundered in by Johan Neeskens put Bulgaria on the run after only six minutes. Rep, again, and Theo de Jong, substituting for Neeskens, doubled the score and it

took an own goal by Krol to beat Jongbloed. It would be the only goal the 33-year-old goalkeeper would concede until the Final. Holland topped Group Three, with Sweden, the other qualifiers, a point behind them.

Holland arguably went forward into the harder group, paired with Brazil, the holders, East Germany and Argen-·na. The East Germans had already enjoyed a unique moment of triumph in winning their first meeting with West Germany, cheered on by 3,000 carefully vetted supporters who had been transported over the Berlin Wall in special trains, while Argentina had inched forward ahead of the highly-fancied Italians. West Germany's consolation at their defeat – and there were cynics who felt it was deliberate – was a place along-side Poland, Yugoslavia and Sweden. On paper it was a less taxing prospect.

If there was one night which encapsulated Holland's contribution it came when the second round got under way on 26 June. In conditions which began in sunshine and ended in a thunderous downpour, the Dutch mastered Argentina. No one was more impressed than those within the game. Brian Clough: 'We'll see no better game than this. The memory of it will keep us warm in the winter.' Derek Dougan was similarly impressed: 'It was breathtaking. The whole Dutch team fitted so well together.' Jack Charlton agreed: 'The Dutch are the complete free-flowing team.' Pat Crerand also saw the value of their numerous talents: 'We knew about Cruyff, but apart from him they've so

Opposite: Brazil's 'keeper Leao punches out against East Germany in their Group A match in Hanover.
Below: ITV's vociferous panel of experts in 3–3 formation with, back row, Clough, Crerand, Dougan, front row, Charlton J., Allison, Moncur.

many other great players. Men like Van Hanegem, Neeskens, Rep, Krol.'

The cause of the adulation was a 4-0 victory in which Argentina were overrun, but, conscious no doubt of their public image as the next host nation, did not resort to cynicism. Cruyff can rarely have played better throughout his glorious career, appropriately making the first incision after only 11 minutes. Krol scored the second, emphasizing the free-wheeling approach that must have disarmed opponents who believed that you could stop the team if you marked Cruyff tightly.

The night had become black and the rain was gushing down when Rep, his blond hair darkened by its soaking, headed a third 18 minutes from the end. The last word, though, belonged to Cruyff who appeared on the left to collect a loose ball in a confused penalty

West German partisans, opposite, warm up for the Final after Beckenbauer, below, had guided his team to a 1-0 victory against Poland in the mud-pools of Frankfurt.

area and make light of a difficult angle for his scoring shot.

East Germany had impressed earlier in the competition with stringent defensive organization but they too could not halt the Dutch who again went ahead with an early goal, Neeskens this time the scorer. Rensenbrink added another in the second half – his first goal in the competition. With Brazil also winning their two games, a genuine semi-final unfolded though the structure of the competition had provided for none. The winner of Brazil's meeting with Holland would be in the Final.

Malcolm Allison by now was enraptured: 'There's no way I can see any team competing with Holland. They are five grades better than any other team. Brazil have no chance against them. Holland are so superior. No way, no way will any other team beat them.' He was right about Brazil.

West Germany had already won their place in the Final, beating Poland on a bog of a pitch in Frankfurt, when Brazil and Holland came to play their quasi-semi-final. The South Americans had not been at their most electrifying but had begun to show their skills in their second-round victories over East Germany and Argentina. But now they attempted to kick their way into the Final.

The Dutch were no innocent angels, but Brazil's violence was astonishingly blatant. Ze Maria, the muscular full-back, announced his intentions with a rugby tackle on Cruyff; Mario Marinho, the centre-back, committed assault on Neeskens in an unsavoury off-the-ball incident. His partner in crime, Luis Pereira, pursued his policy of intimidation until a frighteningly late tackle on Neeskens invoked the red card from the West German referee, Herr Tschenscher.

Holland found the perfect retort

with two goals of the highest quality scored early in the second half. Neeskens timed his run to reach a cross in front of his marker to curve in the first; Cruyff's elegant touch provided the second. The 1974 World Cup was hardly enriched by the tone of the match, but Holland's presence in the Final offered a happy ending to the gruesome spectacle.

Jack Charlton applauded the exit of Luis Pereira: 'He'd got away with murder, this Pereira. But he was finally caught tonight. This was one of the best sendings-off in the competition. Brazil were kicked out of it in 1966 and they've come over this time to make sure it wouldn't happen again. In fact it hasn't been dirty and they've been one of the worst-behaved teams.'

Out in the front line Sir Alf Ramsey concentrated in his report from Germany on the merits of the winners: 'Cruyff is a really great player. He's impossible to stop. He is obviously a star, but he is supported by some very good players, like Neeskens. I don't think I've seen a better player than Neeskens in this competition.'

Johan Neeskens was to be a key figure when the World Cup spotlight switched for the final time to Munich on 7 July 1974. Two years earlier the city had been shrouded in mourning, its Olympic Games shattered by terrorism. Now the Olympiastadion was crammed with those who prayed for a home victory. Holland, a bordering nation, would not lack support as they were to in 1978, but they could not disguise their conviction that it would be an away match. Six of the West German team played for Bayern Munich and knew the ground intimately. But it was a testimony to Holland that the host team were far from being overwhelming favourites.

West Germany's performances had not encouraged optimism. While the Dutch challenge had steadily gathered momentum, the Germans had stuttered. After their defeat by East Germany, they had also been fortunate at times in their group decider against Poland. After Hoeness's penalty had been saved by Tomaszewski, the deadly touch of Gerd Muller had rescued the Germans, whereas Lato, who finished top scorer in the tournament with seven goals, lost his edge when Poland needed it most.

For the Final England were represented on the field by Jack Taylor from Wolverhampton: master butcher by profession, and master of his craft as referee. It was an appointment not without controversy, coming after Scotsman Bob Davidson had announced that the FIFA committee had chosen him to officiate. As Taylor followed out the teams, he noticed that the stage for this most prestigious of matches was shorn of some basic props. The corner-flags which had been removed for the pre-game spectacular had not been replaced. The kick-off of the World Cup Final was delayed while they were found.

The pause might have been responsible for a lack of concentration by West Germany as the players stood back to allow Holland to kick-off, Cruyff and Van Hanegem over the ball. At Taylor's whistle the Germans looked on as the Dutch knocked the ball from one to another as though it was a private practice session. Sixteen passes took the ball back into the Dutch half, forward down their left and back to the centre circle. To Cruyff. No white-shirted player had made contact with the ball or made more than a token challenge as Holland's captain took possession faced by his designated marker, that most harrowing

Franz Beckenbauer, West German national hero, on his armband the powerful word: Spielführer.

The story of Holland's remarkable first-minute goal. Cruyff is tripped by Hoeness, already grounded behind him, and Neeskens thunders his penalty kick past Maier. 'I just concentrated on hitting the ball hard,' he said later.

of defenders, Berti Vogts.

For Cruyff the sparring was over. He attacked Vogts to his left, the defender's right, arrowing forward with his astonishing change of pace. Vogts twisted quickly in his wake, close but not close enough as the Dutchman reached the edge of the penalty area. Only then did another German player break himself out of the watching brief. For the home supporters it was unfortunately Uli Hoeness, a strong-running forward who would not acknowledge tackling as one of his greatest skills. Stretching to his left Hoeness lunged at Cruyff and brought him to the ground, a yard inside the penalty area.

Jack Taylor's first blast on the whistle had been to start the game; his second awarded a first-minute penalty to Holland. Brian Clough called it 'a decision of incredible bravery'. Taylor had no doubts himself, and a re-run of the action confirms the accuracy of his judgment.

Neeskens had already scored from the penalty spot in previous rounds. He knew that Sepp Maier, vastly experienced and professional in his approach, would have studied his technique. Now Holland's chances of taking a crucial early lead depended on a duel with Maier that would be as much one of wits as of skill.

Five years after the event Neeskens was playing for Cosmos of New York, but he could still recall his feelings when Jack Taylor pointed to the spot. 'I was nervous, of course. But not because it was the first minute in the World Cup Final but because it was the first time I had touched the ball.' The recollection provided a fascinating insight into the mental pressures of

playing in the World Cup. Neeskens in fact had been involved in that 16-pass movement, but had been oblivious to it. With the ball on the spot, he did not change his technique.

'Even though I was sure that Maier knew what to expect I just concentrated on hitting the ball hard. I felt that if I did that I would score. The ball went almost straight as he dived to his right, and I really caught it well.'

It was the first penalty in nine World Cup Finals, and only 25 minutes elapsed before the second. To this day Neeskens and all the Dutch players believe that it was inevitable that West Germany would be awarded a penalty to equal the count. Bernd Holzenbein, the 'victim', subsequently admitted that he flung himself to the ground to make the most of a threatening challenge by Wim Jansen.

Derek Dougan's studio comment summed up the dilemma of the referee: 'We're still undecided after looking at it a lot of times. Jack Taylor had to make up his mind there and then.' Later Taylor would reveal that he had penalized Jansen for his 'intent'. 'There's no way he could have got the ball!' Following Hoeness's miss against Poland, Breitner was entrusted with the kick and scored deep to Jongbloed's right.

The rest of the first half belonged to West Germany, with two significant incidents. Helmut Schoen was a manager who had always appreciated the value of wingers, and in Grabowski and Holzenbein he had selected two for the Final. Two minutes before half-time, Grabowski moved forward down the right and slipped the ball to Reiner Bonhof, West Germany's discovery of the tournament. No Dutch cover could

prevent the cross. Gerd Muller's instincts took him to meet it, and the greatest goalscorer of his generation appropriately added the World Cup winner to his tally.

The second incident occurred on the half-time whistle, when Cruyff's one-way conversation with referee Taylor resulted in the yellow card for the Dutch captain who had clearly lost his composure when his side desperately needed him to retain it.

Even with their orchestrator out of tune in the second-half, Holland controlled the play, but the match took on a nightmarish quality for them. Rep twice finished poorly when well placed. Rene van de Kerkhof, substitute for Rensenbrink, drove his shot wide of an open goal, while Maier's superb instinctive save from Neeskens's volley completed the frustration. At the other end Muller

had a goal disallowed for offside, and the combativeness of the Germans shored up the victory.

But through no fault of West Germany a sense of injustice prevailed. Perhaps it was akin to their own feelings when England won with home advantage in 1966. Jack Charlton expressed the mood of many: 'The Dutch deserved to win. They just didn't get what their play deserved. The Dutch 'keeper made one save. Muller had one shot and it went into the back of the net. I can't honestly say that the best team won the World Cup.'

Malcolm Allison, who had pinned a pair of miniature clogs to his lapel before the match as a gesture of support for Holland, was more concessionary: 'When West Germany went a goal down they started to force Holland. They made great runs down the wings which

Before half-time the scoring was over. Breitner equalized for West Germany with a 'return' penalty, opposite, and then the inevitable Muller used one of his rare sightings of the ball to hit the winner, above. By then Cruyff was more than disgruntled by the turn of events and his hot words directed at English referee Jack Taylor earned him the dubious souvenir of a yellow card.

93

was a great tribute to Helmut Schoen. It paid off for him, playing two wingers.'

Brian Clough also had praise for the winners: 'When West Germany got on top the Dutch had no defenders to cope. When the Dutch were on top West Germany had the defenders to cope well. Muller's not had eight chances in this World Cup but he's scored four goals. I was disappointed in Cruyff. He blew up at half-time when he got booked.'

Four years later Johan Cruyff would sit in the same ITV studio and watch as many of his team-mates from Munich reached out for the World Cup and again had it taken from their grasp. Reaching that Final in Argentina was by some criteria an even more impressive achievement, and Rensenbrink's shot that flicked the post at the end of normal-time brought them even closer to success. But though Holland gave

glimpses of their most scintillating form, notably in the 5-1 win over Austria, some of the magic, with Cruyff, had gone. The peak was in 1974.

Holland will not be remembered as winners in the '70s. Even with Cruyff they failed in the 1976 European Championship, finishing third, but our memory of them insists that winning is not all. As Malcolm Allison put it so succinctly: 'Once in a lifetime you see great teams and one of those was Holland.'

The match is over and Beckenbauer holds the World Cup high. Later Helmut Schoen, inset, and Paul Breitner, scorer of the equalizer, held it for a while during the victory jog round the Olympic Stadium. Outside West Germany, many lovers of the game grieved that so talented a side as the Dutch had had to lose. On the ITV panel opinions were divided but none could deny that the Germans had lived dangerously.

THE REVIE YEARS

WHEN MANAGER Don Revie pulled Leeds back into Division I in 1963-64, he taught them to hunger for success. And success meant coming first. Second place was failure, the loser's medal. yet super-professional Leeds were to finish with more second places than any other position in what must go down in history as the club's greatest years.

First, let's count the victories since 1964.

League Championship
Two
FA Cup
One
Football League Cup
One
Victories in Europe
Two (both Fairs Cup)
Total victories: 6
Now for the second places.
League Division I
Five
FA Cup
Three
Runners-up in European Finals
Three
Total seconds: 11.

It's a fine record: 6 first and 11 seconds. But what hounds the perfectionists of Elland Road is what might have been!

NEWS IN BRIEF

■ Incidents in a Danish night club led to life international bans for Messrs. Bremner, Young, Graham, Harper and McCluskey.
■ George Best signed for Stockport Co for one month.
■ Kevin Reeves (Bournemouth) and Kenny Sansom (Crystal Palace) made their League debuts.
■ Derby Co's League title was won with the lowest points total (53) since Chelsea won in 1954-55 with 52 points.

LEEDS FAIL UP FRONT

Leeds came second once again as Bayern made the most of their opportunities in the European Cup Final. Despite having more of the game, Leeds could not break down the Bayern defence. The European Cup-holders bided their time, and sealed the match through Roth and the inevitable Gerd Muller.

It was a bruising game which saw both Andersson and Uli Hoeness off the field with injuries before half-time. Leeds were unlucky not to win a penalty, when Beckenbauer appeared to trip Clark, and their night of gloom was complete when Lorimer netted but referee Kitabjian disallowed the goal.

On this day, too, so-called Leeds supporters dismantled enough of the stadium and the city to make it impossible for the UEFA Disciplinary Commission to write off the damage as the excesses of a few disappointed men.

4-year ban
Twelve days after the Paris riots, soccer's rulers in Europe dropped their bombshell. Leeds were banned from European competition for four years. For the Yorkshire club this was the end of an era.

Already Revie-less, they had produced a rudderless display against Europe's finest — and now their ruddy gormless supporters had shorn them of the chance to compete at the game's top level for almost half a decade. With supporters like that, who needs opponents?

FA CRACK DOWN

IN JUNE the FA issued details of a new system for dealing with players who accumulate penalty points. From next season, they would be banned once they reached 20 points for one, two or three matches, according to the type of offence committed.

Instead of an automatic three-match ban, as at present, players sent off would miss one match and also take 12 penalty points.

Clubs are to be punished for harbouring persistent offenders. Any club whose players between them tot up 100 points will be hauled before an FA commission.

HOME CUP-WINNERS		Scottish FA Cup
FA Cup West Ham 2 Fulham 0	Norwich C 0	Celtic 3 Airdrie 1
Football League Cup Aston Villa 1		Scottish League Cup Celtic 6 Hibernian 3

European Round Up

Leeds' venture to the brink of success in the European Cup is described in our lead story. The Cup-Winners' Cup was certain to be a Continentals-only affair once Liverpool and Dundee United had fallen in the 2nd round. In the Final, at Basle, the Russians Dynamo Kiev beat the Hungarians Ferencvaros 3-0.

The Final of the EUFA Cup, between Borussia Mönchen-gladbach andTwente Enschede, was decided in lop-sided fashion. In the first leg the unfancied Dutchmen (though conquerers of Juventus in their semi-final) held the West Germans to a 0-0 draw in Mönchenglad-bach.

But in Holland the Germans seemed strangely at home. Heynckes celebrated his appearance with a hat-trick, and Simonsen scored two, including a penalty, in a convincing 5-1 victory.

On the morning of 26 January 1975, a bearded tally clerk from South London had lifted the previous day's Cup-tie stories off the back page and put them on the front of the Sunday papers. Dickie Guy of Wimbledon, then in the Southern League, had defied the all-international talents of Leeds United, the current First Division champions. The focal point in his array of brave saves had been to stop a penalty from spot-kick expert Peter Lorimer. Wimbledon, with logic-defying form, had left Elland Road with a goalless draw.

While his team-mates were sleeping off their post-match celebrations, Dickie Guy's Sunday began at six o'clock when Dave Underwood, the former Liverpool, Fulham and Watford goalkeeper, and *World of Sport*'s representative at the game, bundled him into a fast car for the 200-mile journey to London Weekend Television's studios.

Although Wimbledon's hero was a happy and willing subject for our exclusive interview, the throng of Fleet Street reporters and photographers being entertained in the 'Big Match' studios finally brought an air of slight confusion to his smiling face. I leaned over to reassure him that our recording would be over by midday and he and his beautiful wife Josie would be free to go home and see the programme in peace.

'I shan't be able to, in fact,' replied football's man of the moment, 'my television's broken.' Which was how my pleasure of a memorable day was splendidly increased by the Guys, who coincidentally lived in the same London suburb of Bromley, sharing Sunday lunch with the Moore family. All of us enjoyed his triumph together.

Wimbledon's feat – they had toppled First Division Burnley to reach the fourth round, and only a cruelly deflected shot from Johnny Giles beat Guy in the replay against Leeds at Selhurst Park – typified the lasting appeal of Cup football throughout the '70s. For all the sophistication of coaching techniques and tactical knowledge, giants were still slain, and the feats of the likes of Leatherhead, Wycombe Wanderers and Altrincham emphatically added to the flavour of the decade.

Jimmy Armfield, in his first season in succession to Don Revie at Leeds, was just one of many senior managers who came face to face with impending Cup disaster. Of his Wimbledon experience he recalls: 'Everyone expected us to win but I was never relaxed about the game. But to be honest I never felt that they would beat us even if they played in Regent Street or Wimbledon Common, let alone Wimbledon Football Club. I could never see them scoring a goal. After the draw it was to our advantage that the replay was played at Crystal Palace, and I said to the players that all we had to do was to score a goal.'

Wimbledon's ability to compete with players of a higher calibre of individual skills lay solidly in a disciplined man-for-man marking system, fortified by a sweeper, and in exuberant industry. Armfield's players were mystified at times: 'I kept urging Joe Jordan to push up on to their sweeper, but it's very hard to change people's habits. In fact we could have scored 20 even though their defenders and the goalkeeper played so well. In the end the succession of misses had an effect on the whole team and we became too cautious. Take Peter Lorimer. He normally blasted his penalties and had a great record, but now he chose to sidefoot it to the goalkeeper's right . . . just to make sure, I suppose. He dropped on to it easily. But

all credit to Wimbledon. I was very impressed with the way Alan Batsford organized the side and I enjoyed the opportunity during the two meetings to talk over with him the way his team played.'

Though Wimbledon's glory finished in that fourth-round replay, the fairy-tale of Cup upsets continued to the Final itself in 1975. Friendly but hardly fashionable Fulham, the Thameside club who were just keeping their heads above water in the middle reaches of the Second Division, plotted a course that took them to Wembley. Though they were not to share the ultimate satisfaction

Wimbledon goalkeeper Dickie Guy repeatedly beat out all that Leeds could throw at him, including a penalty by Peter Lorimer, below.

of Sunderland in 1973 and Southampton in 1976, the two FA Cup-winners of the decade from Division Two, the romance of their story had a genuine appeal, and, through the fall of the coin that is tossed to decide which channel televises individual Cup-ties, Independent Television enjoyed that journey with the homely team from Craven Cottage.

Much of the romance stemmed from the presence in the Fulham side of Bobby Moore, destined to play in the Final against his old colleagues from West Ham, and Alan Mullery, two

Dickie Guy had good reason to curse his luck when a lucky deflection stole past him in the replay.

ageing great players who dug deep into their experience to bolster the team. But there was also the warmth of goalkeeper Peter Mellor, whose enthusiasm included adding 'Wembley' to the christian names of his new-born son; happy-go-lucky John Mitchell, nicknamed Ted because of his Ted Heath laugh, and Jimmy Conway, an Irish leprechaun who inevitably was the butt of much of the team's humour. In all, they were a squad that gave the lie to the feeling that nice guys never make a mark in the game; they also had Alec Stock, a war-horse in management, providing stability at the top ably supported by the coaching talents of Bill Taylor.

ITV cameras followed Fulham's progress at Goodison Park in the fifth round where Viv Busby, bespectacled off the field, was twice dead-eyed in front of the Everton goal; at Carlisle in round six where Mellor's agility provided the platform for victory and Les Barrett's breakaway goal sealed it; and at Hillsborough in the semi-final where Mitchell's sweetly-struck 20-yarder seemed to ensure a place in the Final for the Second Division sensations – only for Joe Gallagher to scramble an equalizer for Birmingham City.

With West Ham also drawing against Ipswich, the two semi-final replays had to yield full televison coverage to Leeds's European Cup semi-final first leg against Barcelona. Film cameras were nonetheless at Maine Road to capture the drama that finally took Fulham to Wembley. But only just. For much of the match Birmingham justified their First Division status by battering away at Mellor's goal. Gordon Taylor, then in Birmingham's midfield, would say tearfully after the match that Fulham's name had to be on the Cup, so fortunate had they been to survive. Yet Birmingham could not score, and as the game went into extra-time, much of the talk in the stand was about the news of Alan Taylor's two goals that had beaten Ipswich at Stamford Bridge. The alternative topic was picking the venue for the third meeting between Fulham and Birmingham, as the goalless draw seemed increasingly inevitable. Martin Tyler was there and takes up the story.

Three minutes before the end Bob Gardam, who was directing ITV's film coverage, took the decision to move one of our two cameras. There had been no major story to report for *On The Ball* the following Saturday; reporter Gerry Harrison with West Ham would provide much of the Cup material. The referee was already checking his watch as the camera was placed at the mouth of the Maine Road tunnel to film the players shaking hands and walking off. But instantly that scene of resigned calm was enveloped in pandemonium.

John Dowie slung one final cross into the Birmingham goal area where Mitchell's tiring legs carried him on a last run. He made no clean contact but the ball looped off his shoulder past a transfixed Dave Latchford. Just nine seconds of extra-time remained. While the London-based camera crew fought back their own instinctive desire to join in the Fulham revelry rather than record it for posterity, my own reaction was to run back up the tunnel towards the Fulham dressing-room. Now a hundred questions had to be asked in there, and a frustrated reporter had suddenly become a very lucky one.

The celebrations continued throughout the night and, uninterrupted by sleep, onto a nine o'clock train back to London next morning with England's most famous captain, whose impish sense of fun was often kept under wraps in public, leading the revelry.

Moore's humour was to sustain the team through the only nastiness that surrounded Fulham in 1975. On the eve of the Final the calm at their headquarters at the West Lodge Park Hotel in Hertfordshire was disturbed by a dispute over which boots the team should wear at Wembley. I was sitting with the majority of players enjoying afternoon tea when a bailiff served a writ on behalf of an aggrieved manufacturer. Moore took the sting out of the situation with the quick retort: 'Now we've got an outside-writ, an inside-writ

John Mitchell turns in Fulham's winner with nine seconds remaining of the semi-final replay against Birmingham.

and a writ-half!' Indeed Les Strong, the injured full-back, had to represent the team in court on the morning of the match.

John Lacy, 'Blakey' to the dressing-room after the character in *On the Buses,* almost took the fairy-story up to the steps of the Royal Box, but his crisp header in the early minutes of the Final flashed inches wide. Instead the 1975 FA Cup belonged to West Ham, and particularly to Alan Taylor, though a visitor to the post-match banquets, set less than a hundred yards apart in London's Park Lane, would have thought the result had been reversed. Even in defeat Fulham's overt joy at what they had experienced continued unabashed. John Fraser, the reserve full-back who deputized so well first for John Cutbush and then for Strong, epitomized Fulham's lack of cynicism when he thanked reporters for covering the Cup run. The thanks should surely have been delivered from the other side.

With the notable exceptions of Sunderland and Southampton, it is the inevitable fate of the giant-killer that he, like Fulham, is finally slain. Thus in the decade came results like: Everton 5 Colchester United 0 in the fifth round of the 1971 FA Cup, and West Ham United 3 Hereford United 1 in the fourth round of the 1972 competition. Each represented the end of sagas that deserve recollection.

The garrison town of Colchester was an appropriate post for Dick Graham, who utilized his experience as a ser-

geant-major for a distinctive style of football management. Previously a goalkeeper and later manager at Crystal Palace, he inherited a club of humble tradition at the tiny Layer Road ground. Colchester were only elected to the Football League in 1950, and to this day have not performed any higher than the Third Division. But after 13 February 1971 their place in the annals of football was assured.

Around him Graham had collected a number of senior players who had been released from other clubs because of their age. Ray Crawford, a former England striker, bore the most famous name, but others like Brian Garvey, Brian Lewis, Derek Gibbs and Bobby Cram had performed as thoroughly efficient professionals for more years than they cared to remember. John Kurila, mild of manner off the field but a fearsome centre-back on it, had helped Northampton in the '60s in their rise from the Fourth to the First Division.

Garvey, along with Brian Owen, joined Colchester at the start of that memorable season from Watford, where a year before they had been part of a Cup run that had included defeating Liverpool and reaching the semi-final. Owen was sidelined by injury when Colchester met Leeds, but has an incisive recall of Graham's methods.

'The first day of pre-season training is usually a gentle loosener, but not for Dick. On my first day we ran from Layer Road to an army tank training ground and then ran up and down a 300-yard incline for 45 minutes and then we ran back to the ground. In the afternoon he found something approaching a vertical incline and we ran up and down that until we dropped. All this was a regular feature with weight-training thrown in as well. It was almost athletic training, but it kept the older

Ray Crawford heads the first Colchester goal against Leeds with 'keeper Sprake far off his line, having misjudged the cross. Crawford, formerly an international with Ramsey's Ipswich, had another surprise in store for Leeds (see over page).

players playing. We did feel sometimes that the reason we did not do so well in the League was that we had left some of our fitness on the track, so to speak. But it did mean that on any one day we were able to pull out all the stops.'

In the fourth round of the 1970-71 FA Cup Colchester had had to do just that, coming back from three goals down and eventually beating Rochdale after a replay. The effort earned them the right to entertain mighty

Leeds United at Layer Road in the fifth round.

Don Revie's Leeds were now at their peak. Despite their record of near-misses – which included being desperately unlucky as losing FA Cup finalists ten months earlier – their play had developed from suspicious beginnings to reach a quality rarely equalled in the

Crawford lashes No 2 for Colchester after a mix-up in the Leeds defence.

Football League. As well as developing a playing staff glistening with internationals, Revie approached every match with thorough preparation. Unlike more brittle First Division sides, Leeds United were nobody's soft touch.

The media christened Graham's veteran side 'Grandad's Army' as the usual pre-Cup-tie ballyhoo descended on little Layer Road. The Colchester manager entered into the spirit for the visiting pressmen, many of whom were paying their first visit to United's headquarters: he would eat his hat if Colchester won, or climb the walls of Colchester Castle. Above all, Dick Graham was a realist and he knew the disparity between the two sides. Even the 16,000 spectators who crammed into the compact stadium hours before the kick-off had no visions of an upset. They had simply taken the opportunity to see the best team in the country play in their area.

But Leeds were not without a chink in their impressive armoury. Injury kept Billy Bremner out of the side and in goal Gary Sprake, the Welsh international, had been in inconsistent form. For all his genuine ability Sprake was given to momentary lapses and he was not to be at his best in the cramped surroundings of Layer Road. Ray Crawford had made a career out of punishing goalkeepers who were uncertain on crosses, and he was to give Leeds a harrowing afternoon.

Colchester had spent their prematch build-up at a 'lucky' hotel in Clacton. Graham did not travel on the bus to the ground, instead he drove into Colchester with the injured Owen. 'Dick was very, very nervous indeed. He had been putting on a bold front for the players all week, but privately he just hoped that Leeds wouldn't whack us by too many. He really feared an enormous defeat. Actually, though I am sure very few of the players really believed they would win, they never felt that they would not be able to compete.'

Compete they did in a dramatic first-half dominated by Crawford and Sprake's uncertainty. Almost 10 years had passed since Crawford's partnership with Ted Phillips had produced the goals for the shock Championship triumph of Ipswich in 1962-form that for Crawford was rewarded by two England caps. But at 34 he had not lost a radar-like ability to home-in on crosses. After only 18 minutes Lewis began the supply. Sprake misjudged the looping free-kick from the Colchester left, and Crawford headed Colchester into the lead, placing his effort into the junction between crossbar and near-post.

Too much of the game remained for any great show of celebration from the terraces, but Crawford struck again. Sprake, right-back Paul Reaney and the Colchester striker found themselves entangled on the edge of the goal area. As the ball rolled loose Crawford reacted more smartly than his two younger opponents; though lying on his side, he twisted to shoot left-footed into an unattended goal. Two-nil.

Early in the second-half Sprake and Reaney were again left staring at each other when Dave Simmons hurtled on to a hopeful punt from Lewis to touch in a third goal as the two Leeds men hesitated. For Simmons it was a memory to savour in a career which was later broken by cruel misfortune; dogged by cartilage trouble, he fell through a plate-glass window when his knee was strapped and almost died from a severed artery; later he was further handicapped by a serious car accident.

The cavortings that followed Simmons's goal were not lost on match referee Danny Lyden, who admitted later that he had to pinch himself to believe it was really happening. Leeds fought back with goals from Giles and Norman Hunter, and Graham Smith had to make a last-minute save from Mick Jones. It was a dive which ensured Colchester's triumph and took Smith into a prominence that was to earn him a transfer to West Bromwich Albion.

From the touchline Owen was torn between nail-biting and admiration for Leeds. 'Leeds's fight-back was surely one of the most professional performances they have ever given. Even after giving away such bad goals they patiently played their way into the game and nearly came back from an impossible position.'

In the victorious dressing-room it was a painful triumph for John Gilchrist, given the task of shadowing Giles. Leeds had forgotten more about verbal intimidation than Colchester would ever know, and Gilchrist's comment when Cooper miscued a clearance into the stand was downright indiscreet. 'What sort of effort was that from an England full-back?' he yelled. Giles retorted: 'Never mind that, how many caps have you got?' Gilchrist took the bait: 'None, but then I wasn't born in Ireland where they give caps away with packets of cornflakes.' It was Gilchrist who limped off at the end.

But the following season Leeds did win the FA Cup for the first time in a competition which also sparkled with the achievements of Hereford United, who became the first non-League club for seven years to topple First Division opponents. Their achievement won them election to the Football League at the end of the season. To reach the third round the Southern League side had already appeared on a First Divison ground, beating Northampton Town in a second replay at The Hawthorns.

A trip to St James's Park and the resultant share of a large gate seemed ample reward in the draw for the third round. For most of Hereford's part-timers it was a first appearance at Newcastle, and they took the field with these final instructions from player-manager Colin Addison: 'Close them down. If you let Newcastle play in midfield they will murder us.' It took 17 seconds for Hereford to take the lead.

Brian Owen, a burly forward with perhaps not the most delicate touch in the team, burst on to a long pass which flicked off centre-half Ollie Burton's head into his stride. Owen (not the same Brian Owen as the Colchester player mentioned earlier) could have been forgiven if his nerve had failed him in such circumstances but his rasping shot flew into the top corner.

Newcastle's resolution did not crumble, and they bounced back with two goals in quick succession which suggested that they would sweep the non-Leaguers aside. After the match the Hereford players would admit they thought their senior opponents would go on to score six. But Addison, whose service to Sheffield United, Nottingham Forest and Arsenal set him apart as Hereford's most gifted as well as most experienced player, fired in an equalizer from fully 30 yards. The baying abuse from disenchanted Geordies, as much as Hereford's own fighting spirit, put an end to the scoring.

The replay suffered mightily at the hands of the winter weather. Continual postponements hardly helped Newcastle's nerve as a club with a history of disasters against humble opponents. The tie was finally scheduled for Saturday 5 February–the same afternoon that the other Cup survivors were playing in the fourth round. The time-lapse enabled Newcastle to patch

Great moments for Hereford United in the Cup replay against Newcastle. Above, Ron Radford's 35-yarder flies into the net to level the scores. Below, Ricky George (by post) slips the winner past McFaul. Right, Hereford bullocks on the rampage.

up their captain, Bobby Moncur, and he returned to their defence.

Addison was able to announce an unchanged side, which meant that Ricky George travelled to Hereford from his home in Barnet on the Friday night knowing that he would again be the substitute. George, by his own admission, had wasted the chances of a full-time career by a poor attitude. He had been on the receiving end of free transfers from Spurs, Watford, Bournemouth and Oxford. The fact that Addison had paid a small fee to Barnet to bring

Hereford players get out the pomagne in the dressing-room after their win over Newcastle.

him to Hereford had given him a boost, but he had not won a regular place.

That Friday night he and his wife took the opportunity of dining with a long-time friend, BBC Television commentator John Motson, who was covering the match. When they returned to the Green Dragon Hotel it was 10.30. 'I didn't feel like going to bed and I knew I wouldn't sleep, so I stayed downstairs for an hour or so and had a couple of drinks. Nothing serious. But when I finally went to the lift I bumped into Jackie Milburn was was reporting the match for a Sunday paper.

'He really sailed into me, saying it was undisciplined players like me who had made him give up football management. He really took me to task for not being in bed, and didn't really listen when I told him I had in fact drunk very little. To end the conversation I said: "Hang on a minute, I'm only substitute anyway." He said I'd probably come on and score the winning goal.'

Milburn's throw-away prediction proved to be uncannily accurate. Yet with only eight minutes left of a match in which both sides had faced a battle against cloying mud as much as against each other, Newcastle seemed certain to have survived their test. Viv Busby, on loan from Luton, crossed deep from the right. Mick McLaughlin momentarily lost Malcolm Macdonald, virtually his only mistake in the entire Cup run, and Macdonald made his header count.

Addison called for his substitute: 'Come on Ricky, get us a goal.' The sub hardly relished the task. 'What could I do with only five minutes remaining?' he recalled. But the solution came immediately from another quarter. Ron Radford picked up a ball in midfield and played what to all intents looked like a one-two with Owen, though the ball may have rebounded kindly as the tiring forward attempted to control it. Radford arrowed his shot from all of 35 yards past a floundering McFaul. It was only his second goal of the season.

Hereford and Ricky George now approached extra-time with real confidence. 'We all thought when Raddy scored that we would win.' The winning moment belonged to the substitute. 'I remember Dudley Tyler trying a shot

with his left foot that was so mishit it came straight to me like a pass to our right of the goal. Bobby Moncur should have been behind me but I was aware that he had got caught in front. He'd played so well but he'd only just come back from injury and his legs were by then really heavy. I knew the goal was somewhere near and I just tried a shot. It went across the goal and in.'

The defeat affected Newcastle's manager Joe Harvey so badly that on their long journey he stopped the bus to be sick at the roadside. Busby, who had not looked out of place in the First Division side, immediately had his loan cancelled and had to wait four years to reach the First Division on a permanent basis with Norwich and then Stoke.

Hereford went on to draw with West Ham, before losing to a Geoff Hurst hat-trick at Upton Park. Billy Meadows scored for Hereford as their great run closed; it was some reward for the striker whose goals on bleak midweek evenings at places like Nuneaton and Chelmsford had carried the side forward in the Southern League, but who had missed out on the Cup victories.

Both Meadows and George had been released from Edgar Street by the time Hereford began their League career the following August. Addison, too, would leave as the club surged up into the Second Division. But he ended the decade in the top flight, appointed manager of Derby County in 1979.

Wimbledon (and also Wigan Athletic, another successful Cup-fighting side) ended the '70s as Football League clubs – proof that FA Cup giant-killing was not just a self-contained sideshow. The Davids of the decade also received the chance to become Goliaths.

Hereford and West Ham before an over-capacity crowd at Upton Park.

BAYERN BEAT ST. ETIENNE

BAYERN MUNICH held on to the European Cup with a dogged 1-0 victory over French champions St Etienne at Hampden Park. The Frenchmen raced into electrifying attack in the opening minutes and several times went near. But, like Leeds before them, they could not punish the German defence. Bayern clinched the trophy with a second-half goal from Roth.

English entrants Derby Co had begun their second round with a 4-1 home win over Real Madrid, but lost all in the return match, going down 1-5.

In the Cup-Winners' Cup West Ham went all the way to the Final against Anderlecht. But they couldn't beat the Belgians - and their home supporters - in Brussels, and the Cup went to Anderlecht with a 4-2 victory.

Liverpool were Britain's other finalists in Europe. They sailed close to the wind against Bruges, allowing them to score twice at Anfield in the first leg of the UEFA Cup Final. Going to Bruges with a 3-2 lead, Liverpool held on for the 1-1 result that they needed to bring the trophy back to Britain.

IT'S YELLOW FOR 'WATCH IT' AND RED FOR 'OFF'

On 2 October League referees added two cards to their standard equipment. The yellow card is to show the player and the crowd that an official caution has been given and the red to signify instant dismissal.

The practice is the same as before - the names go into the book when players are cautioned and two cautions lead to a sending off. But referees themselves were sometimes in trouble. Failure to flourish a card at the appropriate time brought sharp rebukes from their supporters.

LEAGUE UPS AND DOWNS

Division I
Champions Liverpool, runners-up QPR. Relegated Wolves, Burnley, Sheffield U.
Division II
Champions Sunderland, also promoted Bristol C, WBA. Relegated Oxford U, York C, Portsmouth.
Division III
Champions Hereford U, also promoted Cardiff C, Millwall. Relegated Aldershot, Colchester U, Southend U, Halifax T.
Division IV
Champions Lincoln C, also promoted Northampton T, Reading, Tranmere R.
Scottish Premier Division
Champions Rangers, runners-up Celtic. Relegated Dundee, St Johnstone
Division I
Champions Partick T, also promoted Kilmarnock. Relegated Dunfermline A, Clyde.
Division II
Champions Clydebank, also promoted Raith R.

TRANSFER MARKET

MALCOLM MACDONALD'S move to Arsenal from Newcastle cost the Londoners one-third of a million pounds.

Derek Hales's goal-scoring form for Charlton boosted his market value to a Division II record of £280,000 when he moved up to Derby Co.

In a reshuffle at Ipswich the East Anglians sold striker David Johnson to Liverpool for £200,000 and paid out £200,000 to bring Paul Mariner up from Plymouth.

There was a farewell to old favourites at Leeds. Billy Bremner went to Hull, Norman Hunter went to Bristol City, Terry Yorath to Coventry and Mick Bates to Walsall.

STARS FOR EXPORT

Is Soccer really going to take off in the U.S.A?

A NEW KIND of mobility has seized today's soccer stars. Many are looking to the riches offered in the States. But others have their minds set on becoming Euro-footballers, with a higher standard of living and lower taxes - major inducements.

Duncan McKenzie is taking his brand of artistry off to Belgian club Anderlecht, while Martin Chivers has signed for Swiss club Servette.

In the United States the new dawn has been a long time coming.
- Pele turns out for super-club New York Cosmos, now managed by Ken Furphy, formerly of Sheffield United. When they arrived in West Coast Seattle to play the local Sounders side, 58,128 went to watch.
- Rodney Marsh has signed for Tampa Bay Rowdies.
- Bobby Moore has signed for San Antonio.

Then there was the Bicentennial Tournament, a four-sided contest between England, Brazil, Italy and Team America. England came alive in all three matches, won two of them but could not beat Brazil.

Team America, borrowing ageing stars Pele, Bobby Moore, Chinaglia and Mike England, were fourth. But the interest was there. The crowds came. Boys in schools are wanting to learn the game.

IN THE GOALS

Leading marksman in Division I was Alan Gowling (Newcastle U). Although he only scored 16 in the League, he found the net 8 times in the FA Cup and 6 times in the League Cup for a total of 30. Second was Ted MacDougall, now with Norwich. His total - 28 goals in the League and two Cup campaigns.

Expensive Derek Hales left Charlton after scoring 31 times for them. But these totals were far exceeded in Divisions III and IV. Hereford's Dixie McNeill and Tranmere's Ronnie Moore both hit 37.

What happened when Wim Van Hanegem said 'No red card' to referee Clive Thomas. See page 116

It was, without argument, the most exhilarating and exhausting week of football, possibly in the long history of the game. The European Championship qualifiers – Yugoslavia the hosts, West Germany, Holland and Czechoslovakia – braced themselves to play two semi-finals, a third-fourth-place match and the Final itself.

Every game spilled over with football of vivid skills and goals of indisputable class, there were come-backs that defied logic and the spice of argument was always in the air. Every game required extra-time and the Final itself twisted and turned excitingly through 90 minutes, through extra-time as well and then was only decided chillingly by penalty kicks.

No event could have been better stage-managed and the crowds in the two centres – in Zagreb and Belgrade – had marvellous value for money.

The opening match was in Zagreb between Holland, still with Cruyff in their side and anxious to find some compensation for their World Cup Final defeat two years earlier, and Czechoslovakia, who, like the Dutch, had never won a major national trophy.

Britain's only representative in Yugoslavia was referee Clive Thomas from Wales. But in that first game he made a contribution that was to have its effect on the whole tournament. The prize was a big one and so the control shown by referees needed to match the occasion. In that opening game Clive Thomas set the tone by refereeing firmly and well – but he also had fortitude enough to show the red card to three players. And, when one of them at first refused to go, he was but a few seconds from abandoning the game.

It may seem an unpromising way to start a championship but there is no doubt that the referee's attitude set a pattern for the rest of the week. Players now knew where they stood. They were encouraged to parade their skills knowing that the laws would be enforced with firmness. And the week took off.

It was a day of ceaseless rain in Zagreb and there were even thoughts that the opening match might not be played. After 90 minutes of absorbing football, with the ball zipping over the wet turf, the score stood at 1-1. Anton Ondrus, the massive Czech defender, had scored with a header – and had then put through his own goal for Holland's equalizer.

Mixed with the superb technique, though, was a sad lack of discipline. Indeed Clive Thomas calls it 'the hardest game I've had in my career'. As he puts it: 'The weather didn't help, but neither did the players.' It was a night when six players would receive the yellow card and three the red card.

Men were sliding in as the rain continued to fall and it was never easy for the referee to determine their intentions. How many were deliberate fouls? How many were induced by uncontrollable sliding on a saturated pitch?

But there was no ignoring two bad tackles by Pollak of Czechoslovakia and Neeskens of Holland and, as the game reached towards the 90 minutes, they were sent off.

It was in extra-time, however, that the biggest explosion came. With the score still 1-1, Holland made a thrust through the middle and Cruyff was brought down on the edge of the Czech penalty area. I thought the Dutch appeals for a free-kick were more than justified, but referee Thomas gave a windmill wave of his arms and play went on. No foul.

What made that decision the more difficult for the Dutch to bear was the sight of the Czechs swarming straight to the other end and Nehoda scoring their second goal. It was here that the trouble started.

Says referee Thomas, 'I felt that the tackle on Cruyff was fair though from another angle in the stand it might have looked as though it was not. When the Czechs scored, Cruyff said nothing to me. But remember I had already booked him.

'But Van Hanegem came over to me and said "No goal". As it was said in the heat of the moment I took no action and walked back towards the centre circle. I knew that if he followed me I would have to caution him. And he did follow me back across the half-way line and delayed the kick-off.

'I turned to Van Hanegem and said, "Yellow card". He said, "No yellow card", and continued to show dissent. I then said, "Red card", but he replied, "No red card", and flatly refused to go off.

'My only concern now was how the hell I was going to get him off. I certainly was not going to manhandle him. So I picked up the ball and walked along the half-way line towards the touchline. I was determined to abandon the game if he wouldn't go. But he gradually walked behind me, came to his senses and went.'

Later, Cruyff was to go off injured and play no further part in the championship and Czechoslovakia scored a third goal through Vesely to make sure of their place in the Final. But this was not the last we were to hear of the Dutch during this week.

'Certain people in UEFA thought that I was a bit too strict,' recalls Clive Thomas. 'They thought I should have gone towards the player to caution him. But if he walks away from me I will never run around the ground after a player. They held a special meeting the

next day to announce the suspensions. Van Hanegem was suspended for three games, the others, I think, for one.'

One night later it was the first appearance of the host country, Yugoslavia, against the world champions West Germany in Belgrade. A massive crowd, a perfect summer's evening – and another breathtaking game.

In no time at all the Yugoslavs, playing beautifully, were two goals ahead. Popivoda and Dzajic, that superb little winger, were the scorers and the Germans began to look anxiously at each other.

Once again their inspration came from Beckenbauer, cruising serenely at the back and then pushing forward with one rippling run after another. His every pass was measured to the inch. West Germany's composure returned and with it their long-held ability to turn a cheek against impending defeat.

Now it was goals by Flohe and a story-book hat-trick from substitute Dieter Muller – one Muller filling the shoes of another now that Gerd had retired from international football – that saw the West Germans into the Final against the Czechs.

The match for third place saw a return to Zagreb and another game that kept the momentum going as Holland retrieved something from their defeat there earlier in the week by beating Yugoslavia 3-2. And this with a team that was missing the injured Cruyff and suspended Neeskens and Van Hanegem. It was also a blow for the Yugoslavs, who during that heady opening 20 minutes against the Germans must even have harboured thoughts of winning the championship in front of their own people. Now they were to finish last.

Geels, his blond hair streaming, sped through the middle for the first Dutch goal and Willie Van de Kerkhof added a second. Before half-time Yugoslavia's defender Katalinski pulled one back and in the second half Dzajic scored the equalizer. But it was Geels again who had the last word for Holland in extra-time. It was another memorable match.

So now we looked towards the Final the following evening. Surely the pace would have to drop. Three games . . . all decided in extra time . . . 15 goals. West Germany and Czechoslovakia had plenty to live up to!

That day started painfully. The alarm call shattered the silence of my room in the Inter-Continental Hotel in Zagreb a few minutes before four o'clock. I had reached my bed a little more than three hours after arriving back from the Holland-Yugoslavia match the previous night.

The European Championship Final was still some 16 hours away but before that there was a five-hour train journey across Yugoslavia, a briefing for the army of European television representatives and that settling-in period at the stadium that all commentators require. There's nothing worse than chasing the clock on a day as important as this one was going to be. The match was to be televised live by ITV at peaktime on that Sunday evening.

So why subject myself to such a long train journey? Simply that the country's internal transport system had been stretched beyond breaking-point and frantic inquiries at airline offices the past few days had suggested that there *might* be a seat on a plane for the one-hour flight to Belgrade that morning. On the other hand there might not. It seemed wiser to go by train.

The taxi arrived in time to get me to the station. That was the first worry of the day out of the way. But if I expected deserted platforms and sleepy officials as we waited for the five o'clock express from Trieste to Belgrade, then that was the first eye-opener of the day. The place was alive with families chattering away and looking forward to a few hours in the sunshine of the countryside.

A comfortable journey, a reclining seat, a cat nap that took some of the sting from the eyes. But now I was aware of the hazard all commentators fear on match-day. Clearly I had eaten something the previous night that had put my stomach on edge.

When you are perched high above a football pitch, relief for such problems is rarely at hand. On Wembley Cup Final days, for example, the need for self-control is great before you find the moment and the nerve to take an ancient, clanking lift from the commentary box to the ground floor!

That morning Yugoslavia Railways offered a breakfast – brought to your seat – of hot, spicy sausage, brown bread and coffee. I declined. Instead I watched from the window as we sped through tiny villages, open fields inhabited, curiously, by swarms of magpies ('one for sorrow, two for joy . . .') but I quickly lost count, and tried feverishly to put my internal disorders out of my mind.

The arrival in Belgrade was on time – soon after 10 o'clock. And the television briefing was at noon. This is the time when the local television producer fills in such technical details for the commentators as to when they can expect the slow-motion replays to appear and from which angle, what the pre-match team-captions will tell us, how frequently the score-captions will be shown on our screens and how long after the final whistle they intend to stay on the air. It's the sort of detail that can make the difference between a smooth production for the viewer and one where he sometimes gets the feeling a commentator is exploring the unknown.

Mind you, the plans that are revealed in the calm of a conference room at midday are often lost in the hurricanes of harassment as the kick-off actually approaches. Once, in Vienna, having been assured of a detailed pre-match build-up in pictures and team-captions five minutes before the kick-off, I found myself talking for eight minutes or more over a static long-shot of the stadium with one team-caption being shown a minute before the start and the other one while the game was in progress. And in Belgium once, for some inexplicable reason, the local TV people came without team-captions and even contemplated showing the line-ups from a close-up of a local paper!

In Belgrade everything seemed to be in order. A coach would arrive at the hotel at six o'clock to take us all to the stadium, so it left five hours for me to do my 'homework' on the two teams, to take another nap, freshen up with a shower and nurse my ailing and groaning stomach through the waiting hours.

The coach journey to the ground is always a subdued affair with the commentators imprisoned by their own thoughts and fears. Unlike the journey back, which is always filled with laughter and shouting by men relieved of a burden and now keen to let everyone know their particular verdict on that goal, that penalty and that player.

Now it was the worrying time. Had we done enough preparation? Had we covered all the facts? Would tonight be the night of the horrendous howler? And please let all the goals be clear-cut and leave no doubt as to who had scored them. Not like my heart-stopping experience in the summer of 1979 when within four days I had to pronounce on

two goal-scoring incidents that defied even the probing eye of slow-motion. Was it Alan Sunderland or Brian Talbot who slid in for the final touch to score Arsenal's first goal against Manchester United in the FA Cup Final? Even the camera behind the goal offered no real assistance and only the following day was it given officially to Talbot. And had not Sunderland scored the winner that afternoon I fancy the arguments might still have been raging.

For it to happen once was bad enough for the commentator. But the following Wednesday evening in Switzerland it happened again. This time it was the Final of the European Cup Winners' Cup – again live on ITV – and this time an identical goalmouth situation where it might have been Klaus Allofs who scored for Fortuna Düsseldorf against Barcelona. On the other hand it might have been his brother Thomas! Eventually it was given to Klaus and the incident was lost in a thrilling game won by Barcelona 4–3. But it is the stuff of commentating nightmares.

Another nightmare is when the commentary position is so high and distant that it leaves the players looking like performing ants. The National Stadium in Belgrade is such a place: a huge bowl, an eight-lane athletics track separating the pitch from the crowd and flat, sweeping terraces up to the row of commentary boxes at the topmost rim. Some colleagues use binoculars on these occasions – that is how distant the action is – but I have never schooled myself to do that.

Then followed a check of the commentary position – narrow plywood

Blond, confident and aggressive, Uli Hoeness intercepts at speed early on in the Final against Czechoslovakia. Later he was to be the star of a thousand unwelcome flashbulbs.

cubicles specially built for this occasion – with a microphone, a televison monitor, a set of headphones and room for little else – and a necessary search for the nearest men's room, though by now the absence of food seemed to have quietened my stomach disorder. And I knew that once the game got under way I'd have too many other things to occupy me! Indeed the Yugoslavs put on a spectacular pre-match display of folk dancing, children's dancing, marching bands and an aircraft display that by comparison left Wembley efforts sadly in the shadows.

Soon the players were out to inspect the pitch and quickly after that West Germany's goalkeeper Sepp Maier was out there again, this time going through a pre-match exercising routine that was nothing short of the London Palladium in its inventiveness and agility. He's always done it, no matter what the game. It is a mark of unswerving professionalism that this great character will now be taking with him into probable and tragic early retirement after a serious car accident in the summer of 1979.

In 1976 Maier was at the height of his powers. So too was Ivo Viktor, a stubby little character shorter than most international goalkeepers but who, on this memorable night, was to become one of Czechoslovakia's most distinguished sons.

As the West Germans and Czechs filed out for the game, I think most of us had half a thought that we were about to see something worthy of this amazing week of football. That it rose to such heights of skill, upheaval and drama

Two down after 25 minutes, the Germans looked again to their imperturbable captain Franz Beckenbauer to run at the Czech defence from deep positions and reassert their claims to be the finest team in Europe.

was beyond our most optimistic hopes. What was to come provided the perfect climax for the greatest week in European football history.

The Czechs wore red and were supported to the last man by the noisy Eastern European crowd. The Germans in white would need all their calm and combative spirit to see them through the night. Particularly when, with 25 minutes gone, they found themselves two goals down.

The first Czech goal came after eight minutes and followed a mistake by Berti Vogts. In the course of a season you could usually count those on the fingers of one hand, but now he lost possession dangerously close to his own penalty area. Maier pushed a hard shot away to his left, but the ball was crossed in again and now Svehlik came in deep from the left to ram it home.

Now with 25 minutes gone the Czechs scored again. This time it was Beckenbauer who headed a free-kick straight to full-back Dobias. He hit a shot, without great power to it, across the goalmouth and in front of Maier and the ball crossed the line just inside the far post.

So yet again the Germans had to dig themselves out of a pit. Their football history is littered with such achievements. Remember that two-goal deficit against England in Leon in 1970? That first-minute goal from the penalty spot by Holland in the 1974 World Cup Final? And, of more recent memory for them, that leeway of two goals that had to be made up against the rampant Yugoslavs three days earlier in the same stadium?

Were they equal to it now? Beckenbauer, with his rippling runs from deep, came forward more and more. There was hardly a pass out of place as he provided a source of inspiration to those around him. But could this wound be healed?

Three minutes later we had the answer as Bonhof made a threatening run down the right. His perfect cross was hooked violently in the Czech net by Dieter Muller. Two-one. It seemed at that moment that once more the German story had its familiar plot. But the Czechs, who had never won a major international title, began to respond. Here, Viktor was magnificent in their goal. He was past 30, and coming to the end of a fine career. His work in the next hour was the stuff that men take to their graves.

Viktor made a series of breath-taking saves. I remember one from Flohe that he flew at and pushed round his left-hand post and, the best of all, when he met a free-kick from Bonhof, hit with the power and timing that is his special copyright, and somehow as it rushed past the wall Viktor turned it round the post.

Viktor also seized the luck that came his way that night, as it did when a German shot rolled gently against a post in the second-half and fell back for the 'keeper to pounce with gratitude upon it.

It must be said that the Czechs continued to contribute fully to a night of exhilarating attacking football. They sent defenders – Pivarnik and Ondrus in particular – forward to search out a third goal that would surely extinguish even the fiery competitiveness of the Germans. And Beckenbauer's men continued to push forward in numbers because losing heroically was the only possible substitute for glorious victory.

So we arrived at one minute from the end of normal time when Viktor made his only error of the night. As West Germany advanced once more and the Italian referee Gonella again consulted his watch, and Yugoslavs by the thousand swarmed towards the exits, the Czechs shuffled the ball away for a corner on the left.

Every white shirt was up; every Czech had retreated to save the match in these last few seconds. When the ball came over, for once Viktor was less than positive. He made a weak attempt at a punched clearance, Holzenbein met it at the same time and his header sent the match into extra-time.

I can see it all now and remember well in the confusion how I was unsure whether it was the fair head of Hoeness

or Holzenbein that had got the touch – a good argument for binoculars, perhaps – and only when the slow-motion replay from behind the goal showed a fleeting glimpse of Holzenbein's No 11 shirt was I sure. So the match took one step towards its remarkable climax.

Both sides had their chances in extra-time as the battle continued to swing from one end to the other. The tension had grown and weariness brought its own mistakes. But the crowd loved it and even though the commentators had now been talking, almost non-stop, for two hours nobody was complaining as the final whistle went and we were left to contemplate the last act of the night. Penalties. Five for each side, the first time a major European event had been decided this way.

All the players were shepherded into the centre-circle – except for the goalkeepers Maier and Viktor who were accompanied by a linesman to the left-hand goal as we looked out from the main stand. Everywhere was silent because everyone knew that now this marvellous night must be decided one way or the other in the coming few minutes.

One by one the penalty-takers

The rival goalkeepers. Opposite, the gallant Ivo Viktor seems to bundle aside both Dieter Muller and Bonhof in his determination that 'they shall not pass'. Below, the famously adhesive gloves of Sepp Maier wrap themselves around the ball.

The battle of the penalties. All now rested on the skills of 10 spot-kickers and two 'keepers. Masny of Czechoslovakia took the first kick. He sent Maier the wrong way and steered the ball to the left. 1–0.

The West Germans sent up perhaps their hottest shot, Dieter Bonhof, seen poised to strike opposite below. Bonhof's fierce drive zoomed far to Viktor's left—almost too far, for it struck the post on its way in. 1–1.

Next was Nehoda. His high shot flew over Sepp Maier to restore the lead and moral advantage to the Czechs. 2–1. Clearly the players were coping superbly with the pressure and their fatigue. Who would crack first?

Now the German Heinz Flohe brought West Germany level with a low drive struck with his deadly left foot. The ball arrowed chest-high past goalkeeper Viktor's left and entered the net just inside the post. 2-2.

Again the goalkeepers changed places, with Maier the condemned man. The Czech response was entrusted to Ondrus, the big defender. He approached the ball thoughtfuly and side-footed it along the ground inside the left-hand post. 3-2.

Bongartz, a German substitute, was next. As his team-mates and rivals looked on, above, from their enclave in the centre circle, Bongartz deceived Viktor with a side-footed shot high to his left. Level again. 3-3.

Jurkemic, the fourth Czech, staked all on power and won his critical wager with a stinging drive over the despairing Maier, who had decided a split-second earlier to dive left. The photograph, above, shows how close it was. 4–3.

The score was 0–7 against the goal-keepers when up came Uli Hoeness. True to his reputation, Hoeness lashed the ball hard. . . but high over Viktor's crossbar. Now the Czechs could clinch it with one kick.

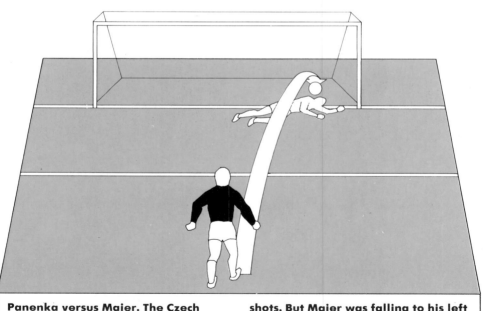

Panenka versus Maier. The Czech moved slowly to the ball, almost went past it and dug in the mildest of chip shots. But Maier was falling to his left and the ball floated over his body into the net. 5–3. It was over.

would march from the sanctuary of that centre-circle to the penalty spot like men condemned. For each it was one kick never to be forgotten - and both goal-keepers were determined to make the memory a painful one.

First to go was Czechoslovakia's Masný, such a skilful prompter of others, but now with a task of his own. He eased the ball past Maier. One-nil. Then it was Bonhof for West Germany. A kick beautifully struck. One-one. Nehoda came next and it was 2-1 to Czechoslovakia. The scoring sequence was un-broken as Flohe made it 2-2.

The nerves of the players were holding under extreme pressure - and it's worth reminding ourselves that these were tired men who had lived on their nerves all night. And now that mighty defender Ondrus scored to put Czechoslovakia in front again by 3-2. It was a kick equalled by Bongartz, who had come on as a substitute. Three-three.

Perhaps we might yet need that provision in the rules that takes the game beyond five penalty-takers for the other six men to enter the argument. Because next to place the ball on the spot was Jurkemic of Czechoslovakia. Again Maier's despairing dive was beaten and it was 4-3.

Now it was Hoeness for West Germany. His blond hair shone under the lights. He looked confident and assured - and that is his nature. He placed the ball carefully. But his shot soared high over the bar and his head was buried in his hands.

The Czechs were leaping about the centre-circle - except for Panenka. He knew the celebrations were a little premature. He still had to get the ball past Maier. If he failed, Hoeness and the whole of Germany would get a reprieve. If he scored, the Czechs would win their first major trophy and his name would be remembered for ever among footballers in his country. Rarely can one kick - or kicker - have been bur-dened by such possibilities.

Would he drive it home? Would

he place it? Maier took a gamble and dived feverishly to his left. But he was beaten by the most curious penalty ever to win so important a championship. Panenka shuffled up to the ball and with a curious little chip shot sent the ball over Maier's body with scarcely power enough for it to reach the back of the net.

Before we - or he - had recovered, Panenka was buried beneath an avalanche of red shirts and Czechoslovakia's triumph was complete. The match itself, for skill, nerve, tension and drama, was never equalled during the decade. Four matches, all of them so keenly contested that all went to extra-time. On the final night a huge television audience had been enthralled from first to last - and one commentator had not given his bad stomach a second thought.

Opposite: The moment of truth as Panenka's chip-shot drifts towards its target. This page: Pivarnik, in a German shirt, holds the trophy; below, the victorious team and their helpers.

Tartan tear-up

FIRST-HALF goals by Gordon McQueen and Kenny Dalglish proved too much for Scotland's over-enthusiastic fans when they came to Wembley for the England match. They controlled themselves while England pulled back to 2-1 through a Mike Channon penalty, but when the final whistle blew, it was the signal for all-out mayhem.

The tartan horde roared onto the sacred Wembley pitch and started slicing it up as souvenirs. They swarmed all over the goalposts and netting, cracked a crossbar and carried off whatever they could.

It was the most unruly behaviour ever seen at Wembley. Damage was estimated by FA secretary Ted Croker at £18,000, and he vowed: 'The ground will be fenced in by November for the Italy match.' For England supporters it was a dismal day — England's second defeat in five days and the fourth that season. The bright lights that had welcomed the Revie era were dimmed.

Three days later England's chances of qualifying for the World Cup finals in Argentina took a steep dive. Italy beat Finland in Helsinki to lead Group I. Kevin Keegan's verdict: England must now win in Luxembourg by double figures, and then beat Italy at Wembley by two or three clear goals.

Thirty-seven days after the defeat at Wembley, Don Revie resigned as England's manager.

A stunned public learned that Revie had already lined himself up a £60,000-a-year job as soccer supremo to the United Arab Emirates. The FA - having spent £25,000 in compensation to Leeds to procure Revie in the first place - reacted angrily.

Rumours had it that Revie was to be banned for four years, but the FA denied this. The pros and cons of retribution were then shelved until a new England manager was found.

To the joy of most, the FA picked Ron Greenwood for the post, for an initial period of three internationals. Next day the FA announced that Don Revie would be charged with bringing the game into disrepute. On 12 December 1977, Greenwood's appointment was confirmed until July 1980.

LEAGUE UPS AND DOWNS

Division I
Champions Liverpool, runners-up Manchester C. Relegated Sunderland, Stoke, Tottenham H.
Division II
Champions Wolves, also promoted Chelsea, Nottingham Forest. Relegated Carlisle U, Plymouth Arg, Hereford U.
Division III

Champions Mansfield T, also promoted Brighton, Crystal Palace. Relegated Reading, Northampton T, Grimsby T, York C.
Division IV
Champions Cambridge U, also promoted Exeter C, Colchester U, Bradford C.
Scottish Premier Division Champions Celtic,

HOME CUP WINNERS
FA Cup Manchester U 2 Liverpool 1
Football League Cup Everton 2 Aston Villa 3 after second replay
Scottish FA Cup Celtic 1 Rangers 0
Scottish League Cup Aberdeen 2 Celtic 1

TRANSFER MARKET

The export of Liverpool's Mr Half-million, Kevin Keegan, to Hamburg over-shadowed all other deals except the one that brought his replacement, Kenny Dalglish, to Anfield from Celtic.

Also on the up were Laurie Cunningham, who went from Orient to WBA for £110,000, and Kevin Reeves, bought by Norwich from Bournemouth for £50,000.

Brian Clough laid in added backbone to Nottingham Forest, acquiring Peter Shilton (Stoke), Kenny Burns (Birmingham), Archie Gemmill (Derby Co) and David Needham (QPR).

WELCOME THE WOMBLES

SOUTHERN LEAGUE Wimbledon - the giantkillers of 1975 - were the popular choice to succeed to the Fourth Division for 1977-78. They took the place of Workington who failed to be re-elected at the Annual General Meeting of the Football League.

Dickie Guy, Wimbledon's heroic goalkeeper in that Leeds FA Cup saga, had repeated his astounding form in a 3rd round replay against Middlesbrough earlier in the season.

And now he and his team-mates at Plough Lane were eager for the challenge of league football under the guidance of manager Allan Batsford. Hereford had shown that Division IV could be a springboard to higher things. But first of all Wimbledon would have to perform against regular league opposition - clubs like Huddersfield and Northampton, who could still remember their days in Division I. And clubs like Halifax, Hartlepool and Southport - the three that finished above luckless Workington.

NEWS IN BRIEF

■ Scotland beat Wales 2-0 to qualify for World Cup finals.

■ Ian Callaghan played his 800th game for Liverpool.

■ Manchester U were ordered out of the European Cup-Winners' Cup because of fans' unruly behaviour in the away leg. They were readmitted after an appeal, but fined £7,500 and obliged to play the return leg 300km from Manchester.

The Liverpool coach drew away from Wembley that sunlit afternoon and the men inside it, more used than most to the noise and celebration of victory, were silent. Liverpool had just been beaten in the FA Cup Final by Manchester United. Now they were on their way back to Merseyside to lick their wounds, analyse their failings and try to restore their spirits before they had to face Borussia Mönchengladbach in the European Cup Final in Rome four days later.

It was a short first journey through London's northern suburbs to catch the north-bound train at Watford. I was with them for that journey, our television camera, its lights, microphone and technicians all part of an arrangement made with Liverpool two weeks earlier but now surely nothing more than instruments of gloom.

Or so it seemed. Yet within a mile of Wembley - where Manchester United were still celebrating the end of a season and their 2 - 1 victory - Liverpool's players had already got their colour back and voice enough to talk optimistically of the next important date in their season.

'Just wait till Wednesday night,' said Ray Clemence. 'Mönchengladbach will pay for this.'

'Our season has not fallen apart because of this one result,' said manager Bob Paisley, the mature voice of good reason. 'We are still the great side we were at three o'clock this afternoon. And these lads have played too long and at too high a level for them to brood about the result. They'll lift themselves by Wednesday night.'

There was a 20-minute wait at Watford for the players, their wives and girlfriends before their train pulled in.

Time to read newspapers that told of what they had left behind that afternoon. But only those privileged to be with them knew that the next chapter had every chance of being altogether more glorious. A performance that outstripped all others in 1977 . . . and even beyond.

One man who was missing from the party was Kevin Keegan. It was at this time that a move to Hamburg had become more than a possibility, and the end of his six years at Liverpool more than a probability. But Keegan was certainly in the Liverpool party, wearing their distinctive all-red strip for the last time it seemed, in the Olympic Stadium in Rome that following Wednesday night.

And what a farewell it was. Keegan gave as complete an individual performance as I can recall, matching those of Stanley Matthews in the 1953 Cup Final, Alfredo di Stefano in the 1960 European Final, and even of Pele during the 1970 World Cup.

It was a hot night but Keegan hustled and tackled, passed and ran, and above all inspired the whole Liverpool team to a masterpiece that was near to flawless in its execution and right at the limit of physical effort.

Yet Keegan was playing his most important game of the season in front of critical men from many clubs (Hamburg uppermost among them) who sought an answer to whether he was worth the half-million pounds Liverpool wanted for him. And in Mönchengladbach's Berti Vogts he faced arguably the best defender in the world. Not least, he needed also to leave with a performance worthy of his time at Anfield.

In the event he left Vogts gasping in his wake almost to the point of embarrassment. And when the little German chased him with despair from the right touchline into the Mönchengladbach penalty area and pulled him

133

down for a penalty in the second half, it proved to be the killing moment of the night.

Keegan was the talk of Europe, his future now highly profitable and beyond doubt. And Liverpool were, for the first time, champions of Europe. It more than compensated for the loss of the treble—the First Division championship, which they had already won, the European Cup, now safely theirs and the FA Cup snatched from them the previous Saturday by Manchester United.

More than that, it provided a marvellous fillip for British football. These were gloomy times. It was nine years since an English club (Manchester United in 1968) had won the European Cup, though Leeds had reached the Final in 1975. England had failed to qualify for the 1974 World Cup and, having already lost to Italy in Rome, seemed destined to watch once more in 1978. Football nations still spoke of England as the nation that had taught them the game, but they were doing it with a smirk on their faces.

Now Liverpool had come up with an answer. And it was one that was exciting and full of football invention and skill. There was nothing more satisfying on this memorable night than Liverpool's opening goal scored by Terry McDermott. The build-up was down the right-hand side and when the ball reached Steve Heighway the German defence had half an eye on a great burst further down the line by Ian Callaghan. But Heighway cut inside, released a pass to the strong-running McDermott, who must have covered 50 yards in that move, and McDermott steered the ball powerfully wide of Kneib in the Mönchengladbach goal. Swift, simple, ruthless—a typical Liverpool goal.

The score was unchanged into

Terry McDermott finds the net for Liverpool's first goal in the Rome Final of the European Cup and, right, begins his victory sprint back upfield.

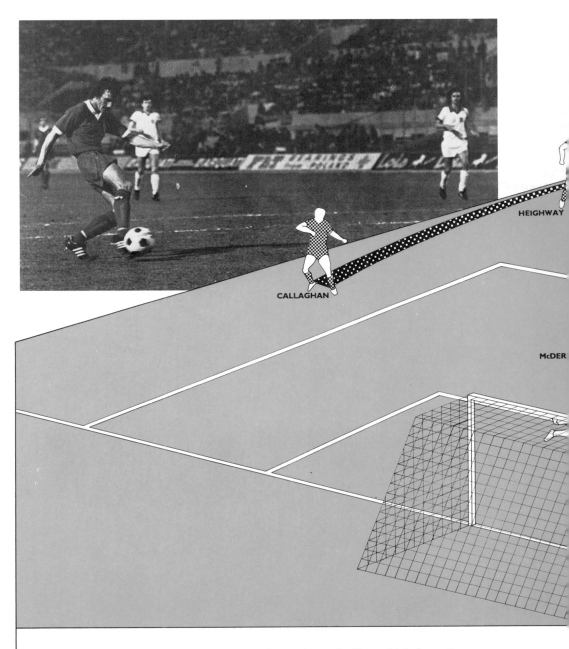

CALLAGHAN

HEIGHWAY

McDER

How McDermott connected and put Liverpool ahead. The move began with Heighway taking a pass down the right-hand side. Callaghan made a dummy burst down the line which drew German eyes to him while Heighway dashed inside. Heading goalwards, he released the ball forwards into the critical space

CALLAGHAN

HEIGHWAY

McDERMOTT

inside the Mönchengladbach penalty area. The Germans had no answer as McDermott arrived on the end of a 50-yard run, collected the ball and fired it across Kneib's dive into the far corner. 1–0. Simple, fast and ruthless, it was a goal typical of Liverpool at their best.

the second half until Liverpool's first mistake was fully punished. They lost the ball some 10 yards outside their own penalty area and Allan Simonsson flashed a surprise shot across Clemence and into the far corner of the Liverpool net.

Would Paisley's machine now crumble? Would their brilliance to this point now be jolted by memories of their Wembley disappointment? Would the Germans, always such superb competitors, now push the door wide open and steal the trophy? All were agonizing questions for English supporters, but Liverpool came up with the best possible set of answers.

After a corner on the left, there was Tommy Smith heading beyond Kneib to put Liverpool back in the lead. Tommy Smith! His fearsome tackling had saved many a goal, but his talents

rarely had been seen at the other end. If this was the veteran Smith's way of saying goodbye after so many rumours of retirement (although he was to play on for another season at Liverpool), it was then equalled by Keegan's. Because now came his run, and the penalty, and the chance for Liverpool to put the match beyond doubt.

Phil Neal, the full-back, came forward to take it. Even now the memory causes him to swallow.

'It was almost too much for me to pick up the ball and put it on the spot,' Phil recalls. 'I knew that if I scored they would be dead, and if I missed it would give them the momentum to get right

Below: The Germans equalize from Simonsson's snap drive.
Opposite: The Keegan-Vogts duel warms up, but the Liverpool man was always faster.

back in the game.

'I remember looking at their goalkeeper . . . I can't remember his name, and thinking he must stand 6 feet 4 inches tall. He blocked out the entire goal. I'd taken a penalty in the semi-final in Zürich and hit it to the goalkeeper's left. So I decided to hit this one to the other side. The 'keeper must have studied that particular kick on television because he dived the wrong way. It was the most important single kick in my career – and there was that lovely ball in the back of the net. It was a glorious moment.

'I've seen so many pictures of that goal but my favourite is the one that shows Ian Callaghan behind me with his hands together as though he is praying. He'd won everything in football apart from a European Cup medal and it was as though he was saying "Go on Phil, stick it in and finish it off." I was glad to do it for him.'

So Phil Neal had produced the final punch and Keegan had provided the muscle. Keegan looks back on the match, naturally, with particular pleasure. 'I think it was one of my very best games,' he says, 'when you take into consideration the occasion, the fact that I was playing against Berti Vogts and that people had to come to see what I was worth.'

That match cemented a special relationship that Keegan now has with Vogts. 'I consider him the greatest professional I've ever played against,' says Keegan. 'And he's one of the nicest men in football. I think if everyone in football – or in life – were like him, it would be a better world to live in.

Tommy Smith makes his unbargained-for appearance in the German box to turn in a Liverpool corner. Note the Keegan-Vogts battle for position on the left of the picture.

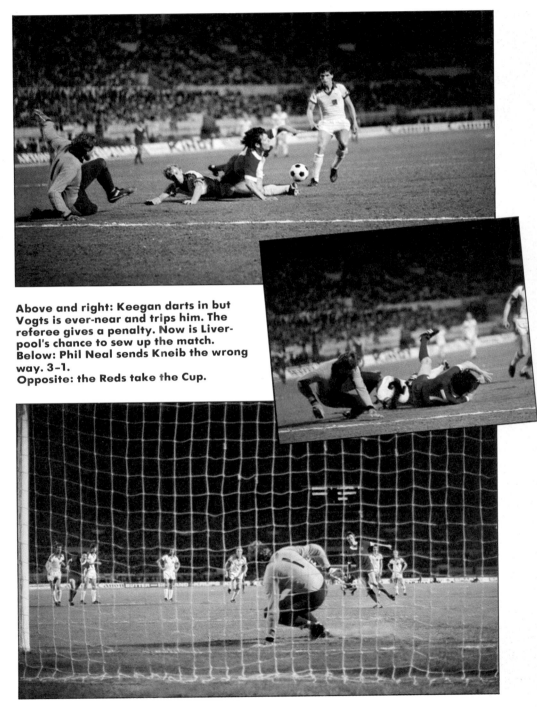

Above and right: Keegan darts in but Vogts is ever-near and trips him. The referee gives a penalty. Now is Liverpool's chance to sew up the match.
Below: Phil Neal sends Kneib the wrong way. 3–1.
Opposite: the Reds take the Cup.

'After that game in Rome, Berti went back to his hotel and must have been right down in the dumps. After all, he'd never won a European Cup medal and now I'd given him a difficult night and made him give away a penalty. But later on that night he came across to our hotel to have a celebration drink with me.

'Mind you, he did also ask me if I was interested in joining Mönchengladbach, so perhaps there were two motives in his gesture. But I could never have done it. I wish I could but I'm a very bad loser. For me there's only one thing – winning.'

And after six years of winning with Liverpool, Keegan was moving on. The year leading up to this triumph in Rome had been far from happy and it is worth recording his problems and setting them against that final, victorious night. He had told Liverpool and their fans a year before that he would play only one more season with the club. He needed a new challenge and after scaling so many peaks with Liverpool the next move had to be abroad.

His honesty brought its problems. As he says: 'The last year at Liverpool was hell for me. It convinced me that people everywhere are fickle. In six years I had run millions of miles for the club and yet towards the end the crowd, who had been marvellous to me for five years, were looking for my every mistake.

'I actually had one Liverpool supporter who came up to me after we had lost the FA Cup Final to Manchester United and swore at me saying that I had not tried a leg. Yet I had run everywhere in that match. I felt so down and I

Liverpool take their vast pot on a tour of the stadium. Keegan at first wanted to duck the ritual, and is missing here. But they got him out in the end.

felt if that was the general opinion of Liverpool fans I would be so disappointed because I think they know me better than that.

'I've never been so totally dedicated to one club as I was to Liverpool. I was just crazy about the club until that last year and even then I always gave them everything I could.

'But it did go a little bit bitter and I just wanted to get away at the end of that season. By now I had agreed to sign for Hamburg and that was the next thing that mattered to me. And after that win in the European Cup I couldn't even be bothered to go and do a lap of honour with the lads. I had to be dragged round by one of the other players. Just

running round with the Cup didn't interest me. Imagine that.'

So Keegan moved on to more success with Hamburg. Liverpool bought Kenny Dalglish with the Keegan money and he scored the winner in the European Cup Final the following season. But it was in Rome that Liverpool showed the world their unique class that stamped them as Britain's most formidable club through the 1970s.

If the Liverpool slogan opposite is a little unclear, we think it says: JOEY ATE THE FROGS LEGS/MADE THE SWISS ROLL/NOW HE'S MUNCHING GLADBACH. Below: Terry McDermott and Emlyn Hughes take the Cup to their fans.

THE GAZETTE

FOREIGN INVASION

IN JUNE we hadn't heard of some of them. But by September we were all crowing about their marvellous gifts. In the forefront were the South Americans: Ardiles, Villa, Tarantini, Sabella. Close behind them came the flood from the Continent, even from behind the Iron Curtain with Manchester City buying Kazimierz Deyna from Legia Warsaw.

The great influx began while we were still getting over that three-week heart-stopper in Argentina, otherwise known as the World Cup. Suddenly word broke that Tottenham manager Keith Burkinshaw had stolen in and snaffled the signatures of two of the World Cup-winning squad.

While the dazed British public was still wondering whether you didn't need forbidden ration books to buy foreign players, the Department of Employment gave the nod and suddenly Osvaldo Ardiles and Ricardo Villa were Spurs players.

Then Alejandro Sabella, another Argentinian, signed for Sheffield United, and Birmingham got Alberto Tarantini .. yes the same Tarantini who scored that crucial second goal in Argentina's World Cup semi-final against Peru.

Meanwhile the European market was buzzing with English buyers. From Partizan Belgrade, Ivan Golac signed for Southampton. The

Polish international Kazimierz Deyna agreed to go to Manchester City. Arnold Muhren joined Ipswich from Dutch club Twente Enschede. There might have been more transfers . . . but deals linking Middlesbrough with Argentina's Houseman, and Birmingham with Brazil's Dirceu failed to go through.

England manager Ron Greenwood praised the inrush of overseas talent. 'They have created a feeling of expectancy, excitement and glamour,' he said.

TRANSFER MARKET

LIVERPOOL WERE in the news at both ends of the market. Quietly a number of veterans moved away from the Anfield and joined up again under John Toshack at Swansea. In the roster of Liverpool Old Boys were Tommy Smith, Ian Callaghan, Phil Boersma and Alan Waddle. They were in part replaced by Graeme Souness, bought for a record £352,000 from Middlesbrough, and Alan Kennedy from Newcastle.

Two Scots made a considerable dent in Manchester United's bank account. They were Gordon McQueen and Joe Jordan, both from Leeds, and in the combined deal more than £800,000 changed hands.

BOB LATCHFORD (Everton) won a £10,000 prize for being the first player from Divisions I and II to score 30 goals. He ended the season with 32. No other player from the top two divisions reached the prize-winning mark.

Two players in Division IV bettered Latchford's total.

NEWS IN BRIEF

■ Kevin Keegan (Hamburg) was voted European Footballer of the Year.
■ Rangers pulled off the Scottish treble of League, Cup and League Cup.
■ Jock Stein became manager of Leeds but left after 45 days to take over the Scottish national side.
■ Non-Leaguers Blythe Spartans had a fine FA Cup run, beating Stoke and reaching the fifth round.

HOME CUP WINNERS	
FA Cup Ipswich T 1 Arsenal 0	
Football League Cup Nottingham F 1 Liverpool 0 after	replay

Scottish FA Cup Rangers 2 Aberdeen 1	
Scottish League Cup Rangers 2 Celtic 1	

SUPER REDS DO IT AGAIN...

ON 10 MAY Liverpool made themselves British club of the decade by beating Bruges 1-0 to take the European Cup for the second year running.

They didn't sparkle in that Wembley Final as they had done in Munich in 1977, but much of the responsibility for the low scoreline

must go to Bruges' 'keeper Jensen, so brilliant on the night.

On their way to the Final, Liverpool were spared from competing in the first round and then devastated several more-than-worthy opponents. Here are the two-leg

aggregates:
2nd round Beat Dynamo Dresden 6-3.
Quarter-final Beat Benfica 6-2.
Semi-final Beat Borussia Mönchen-gladbach 4-2.

In the League, Liverpool finished second to Brian Clough's

Nottingham Forest. This made them runners-up three times in the last five seasons - and winners twice. An incredible record.

All credit, though, to Forest. They also set a new record by becoming the first side to carry off the League and

League Cup double.

The League Cup trophy was especially difficult to win, and had to be decided in a replay, which Forest won narrowly 1-0 with a Robertson penalty. Forest's opponents were, of course . . . Liverpool.

As fiction its melodrama would have been too unbelievable. As fact, even today, some still doubt its validity. As a match it encapsulated the heady atmosphere of the 1978 World Cup more than the Final itself.

This is the story of 21 June 1978, the night when Argentina needed to score four goals – a vast number in the context of an international match – against Peru to qualify to meet Holland in the Final. What followed produced cynicism or exhilaration, depending on your viewpoint.

It should have come as no surprise that the match of the tournament would be surrounded by controversy. Argentina '78 had been built on bricks of debate. Johan Cruyff, you remember, was the most illustrious of several players who dropped out of the World Cup, fearful of their safety in a country subjected to a military dictatorship and perpetually on the brink of civil uprising. I'm sure I was not alone amongst journalists covering the finals in being asked, on moral and humanitarian grounds, not to accept the assignment. So unsettling was the continual anti-regime propaganda that a sense of misgiving was near the surface when the ITV party touched down at Ezira Airport, Buenos Aires on 24 May.

Those misgivings had long since become laughable by the time Argentina were to play Peru in Rosario. There will always remain the slight suspicion that we were all victims of a stunningly successful exercise in public relations. After all, reporters had arrived back from the 1936 Olympic Games full of warmth for Germany. Yet the welcome in Argentina was genuinely overwhelming. Public smiles could have been painted on by order, but not the unending invitations to private homes, not the taxi-driver who refused payment simply because I was covering the World Cup. Add to that the best fillet steak on every restaurant menu for around £1 and you can understand that the standard of living was patently palatable for the British pocket.

Argentina in 1978 was a young country seeking an identity. The people were using football as the solution, which explains the compelling extrovert passion which followed every result, but which would reach new heights on the night of 21 June in Rosario.

Of course, the action that day was not confined to Rosario. In the late afternoon in Mendoza, in the foothills of the Andes, Brazil's Group B encounter with Poland put Argentina's task into perspective. Brazil's coach Claudio Coutinho had protested – with great justification – that the two games should be played simultaneously. FIFA found enough excuses to deny the request: Argentina's games throughout the tournament had been played in the evening, no other games were scheduled then because no one would go to watch, Argentina could not switch to the afternoon because the populace would be at work, and the television companies had made their technical preparations for the original kick-off time.

Brazil still managed to set Argentina a real target. Against a Poland side which also could still have reached the Final with the right combination of results, the Brazilians survived the loss of Zico – a key forward – who was carried off after only three minutes. Nelinho hit a massively swerving free-kick to open the score for Brazil, only for Lato to poach an equalizer on the stroke of half-time. In a stirring second-half, Brazil beat a tattoo on Polish woodwork before

Preço para formação de 22 craques?
$ CR$ 115.000.000,00?

COUTINHO ESTÁ CERTO 1%?

TECNICO

VERGONHA!
PREGUIÇOSOS OU INCOMPETENTES?

Última Hora

Povo exige uma satisfação

Torcedor decepcionado se matou após o jogo

Roberto diluted some of the frustration. Both his goals were reflex shots when the ball ricochetted to him from the post. Three-one to Brazil. The subsequent mathematical exercise showed that Argentina needed four goals. Now Rosario became the focal point of the football world.

I had been commentating there throughout the first round, when the city had been the base camp for secretive Poland, for the splendid outsiders Tunisia and for Mexico, so friendly but sadly the real wooden-spoonists. Sited on the River Parana (Parana fish are a local delicacy and not to be confused, as one illustrious television producer did, with piranha fish), Rosario is similar in size and spirit to Southampton or Middlesbrough with a dockland industry and a non-metropolitan flavour. Imagine, then, the impact of England playing what boiled down to a World Cup semifinal at the Dell or Ayresome Park. Sprinkle in that Argentinian passion and you can appreciate the effect of the arrival of Cesar Luis Menotti's squad in the provinces.

That they were there at all reflected an uncertainty in their progress reminiscent of England's early stutterings in 1966. After narrowly beating Hungary and France, they were upset by Italy. Bettega's elegantly worked winning goal ensured that in the second round Argentina would not have the sanctuary of the River Plate Stadium, their own Wembley. They had to decamp for Rosario.

One school of thought maintained that defeat had actually worked to Argentina's advantage. Now they would play in Group B-away from West Germany, the holders, Holland, and, of course, Italy. Their opponents-on paper at least-presented slightly fewer alarms. Traditionally Brazil are not the obstacle to their South American rivals that they are to the rest of the world. Peru would not provide an unknown quantity, while Poland had the bonus of two first-round matches in the city but had upset the locals by not allowing public access to training sessions. The stadium itself, refurbished but still only holding 40,000, had a British-style compactness which would only make the fanatical support still more intimidating for the visitors.

Argentina arrived in their new camp on 12 June, two days before they were to start their Group B schedule by meeting Poland. That day I was in Cordoba, two hundred miles further north. In the morning, ITV and BBC officials put their heads together to work out which channel would cover which matches in the second round. Only after that meeting did John Bromley, ITV's controller-in-chief in Buenos Aires, allocate commentators to matches. It was lunch-time before I was told of my personal roster which began with Argentina v Poland, and it was late evening before I arrived back in Rosario.

At that time I had not seen Argentina play, so I was looking forward to watching them train on the day prior to the game to make sure of my identifications. Unfortunately Cesar Luis Menotti did not share my enthusiasm. Press access to the camp was banned - particularly alarming news because the outline numbers on the Argentinians' blue and white striped shirts were indecipherable. Kempes and Luque, moustachioed and with flowing black hair, were often indistinguishable.

The sour taste of failure, South American style. A voodoo doll representing the Brazilian coach Claudio Coutinho hangs from a scaffold, and a placard screaming 'Shame! Lazy or Incompetent?' berates him for Brazil's shaky start in the 1978 finals.

Unquenchably optimistic, I duly turned up at the camp, but polite requests which later became beseechings were rebuffed by a succession of press officers and security guards who added to my considerable collection of team pictures but whose resolve to keep me on the outside did not weaken. When I finally found a fence to peer through with binoculars, Menotti himself strode across the training ground in my direction. You did not need 'O' Level Spanish to get the drift of his comments, reinforced by more guards who were supposed to move me on. Panic at not being able to do my job the next day rather than bravery forced me into a confrontation but I stumbled upon the solution. 'I go home and tell everyone Argentinians no amigos,' was my last retort. Totally unfair and inaccurate as that was, the message worked. World opinion was a sensitive area, and I was allowed to stay and watch.

My good fortune did not end there. Those unforgiveable numbers were altered, and Mario Kempes, seeking a change of luck in the search for his first goal in the World Cup finals (he'd also failed to score in West Germany in 1974) shaved off his moustache. I then heard from my own HQ that I was to stay with Argentina throughout the second round. A combination of fog in Buenos Aires and storms around the country threatened the air services which were the key to inter-city communications. I had been scheduled to move on to Mendoza to cover Brazil v Peru and then to Cordoba for Austria v West Germany. Hugh Johns, Gerald Sinstadt and Gerry Harrison were all on similar circuitous routes. Now we were all to stay put, and that is how I came to see Argentina's confrontation with Peru.

Before the tournament the Peruvians themselves had been as secretive as Menotti at times chose to be, especially to the British, fearing us all to be spies from Scotland, their first opponents. Certainly no genuine spies from Scotland appeared to have learned any secrets when Ally MacLeod's side was overrun by Peru's skill, particularly in midfield where Teofilo Cubillas's two goals emphasized his contribution, and on the flanks where Juan-Jose Munante and Juan Oblitas stretched Scotland to breaking point. By dint of a 0-0 draw with Holland and a resounding 4-1 victory against Iran, Peru topped Group Four, as inspired as they had been in reaching the quarter-finals in 1970. With their new confidence, suspicion disappeared, and smiles and friendly hand-

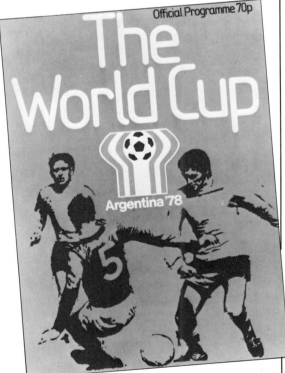

Official Programme 70p

The World Cup

Argentina '78

Cover of an English-language preview programme. Inside, much play was made of Scotland's chances, but Ally MacLeod's men were outrun by Peru.

shakes, and from Cubillas a little halting English, awaited reporters who crossed the path of their party.

In that party was one player crucial to the story of 21 June. Ramon Quiroga, a month short of his 28th birthday, was Peru's regular goalkeeper. His cavalier and at times eccentric style – his charge to the halfway line to rugby-tackle Poland's Lato remains one of the most bizarre incidents of the World Cup – earned him the nickname of *El Loco*, the Crazy Man. His eccentricities would have merely added to the colour of the occasion, but for one other significant factor.

Ramon Quiroga had only been a Peruvian for one year. A naturalized citizen, he had been born in Argentina; furthermore, he had been brought up in Rosario, and he had joined the junior ranks of the Rosario Central Club as a 13-year-old. In 1969 he made his debut in the First Division and three years later he had been transferred to Sporting Cristal in Peru. By 1976 he had returned to Argentina, and played for Independiente, but it was a brief hiatus. After transferring back to Sporting Cristal the following year, he took out Peruvian citizenship, and immediately followed another Argentinian goalkeeper, Humberto Ballesteros, into the national side. The irony remained inescapable. In a situation where goals were crucial, the main barrier to Argentina's progress to the Final was to be a man who in almost every respect was Argentinian himself.

When Peru arrived in Rosario after playing against Brazil and Poland in Mendoza, I sought out Quiroga after training. Would he want to play at all? After all, Peru had two other healthy goalkeepers in their squad, 32-year-old Ottorino Sartor and Juan Caceres, the player finally allocated Number 13 after the superstitious Peruvians had tried to

persuade FIFA to allow a Number 23 instead. No one would blame Quiroga if he chose to stand down in a situation that could be regarded as invidious.

He understood the logic of the question but denounced it. 'Of course I want to play. I am a Peruvian now and I am very proud of it. If I am selected I will want to do my very best. Argentina are the opposition just as Poland have been. And Brazil. And every other country.' The words were jumbled but the message was clear. When the cynical inquests were on everyone's lips after the game, it was hard to lay direct blame at Ramon Quiroga's door.

The mood Peru now found themselves in is particularly relevant to the events of 21 June. After raising their game to all-conquering heights in the first round, they had understandably shown adverse reaction in Group B. Brazil, a resolute and a philosophically less flamboyant side in 1978, carried too much weight for them. Dirceu, from long range with a lancing free-kick and a less explosive effort that slipped under Quiroga's body, scored two goals that more than settled that match. They pricked the Peruvian bubble. Zico's late penalty simply boosted Brazil's goal difference.

A reverse of similar proportions should have followed against Poland, and had it happened fewer eyebrows would have been raised three days later. Instead, the very best of Quiroga and some slipshod Polish finishing restricted the beating to a single goal, scored by Szarmach, who at last revived memories of his power of 1974. Make no mistake, however, this was a totally one-sided affair.

In terms of morale, therefore, they were far from the same Peru who had cavorted in delight after destroying Scotland. Nor could they bring to their clash with Argentina the same level of fitness. The big, black centre-back Rodolfo Manzo was only passed fit from a leg injury on the morning of the game, taking his place alongside the veteran Hector Chumpitaz, whose declared age of 34 was open to question. Manzo might not have played at all had Peru's defensive back-up not been badly weakened by injuries to full-backs Toribio Diaz and Jose Navarro. Twenty-two-year-old Roberto Rojas was named at left-back, his first game in the tournament, and his inexperience was to be cruelly exploited. Further forward Juan-Jose Munante, the impressive winger with a sprinter's pace, had come off against Poland suffering from a stomach upset. And it would be stomach Peru would need most against Argentina, who had lost just three of the 23 meetings between the countries.

Argentina had experienced their scares in Group B, but until they knew they would need that four-goal margin, there had been little to undermine their self-confidence. Against Poland they had produced two heroes. The clean-shaven Kempes finally broke his World Cup duck with a crisp header before the first quarter of an hour had passed. Then his agility was tested at the other end, pawing the ball off his own line at the cost of a penalty.

Poland's captain, Kazimierz Deyna, had then ruined the night of his 100th international by failing to outwit Ubaldo Fillol. The save in isolation was undramatic from a tentative shot, but in its context was sensational. Fillol had previously conducted a feud with Menotti that severely threatened his presence in the squad; now his status was unquestioned, the save reinforcing his general excellence throughout the competition. Kempes's second goal sealed the win, 19 minutes from time, when Ardiles

thrust forward to create the chance.

It now became crucial for Argentina not to lose to Brazil. Statistically they carried into the game one of the few plus-records in internationals against Brazil, but current form was a more relevant guide. Argentina had lost their last five meetings and not won in the previous eight. Brazil could even point to a win less than three years earlier in Rosario, by one goal to nil. They also passed another landmark on the night, becoming the first country to reach 50 ties in World Cup finals. Only nine of the previous 49 games had ended in defeat.

They did not lose the 50th either. But neither did Argentina. The goalless draw had all the prettiness of an alehouse brawl, the stalemate illustrating again the physical play of the Brazilians – unflatteringly called a 'Europeanizing' style by Brazil's coaches who had seen their pre-World Cup tour of Europe as a toughening process. Argentina's discipline throughout the competition, in the light of their previous record of violence, remained remarkable and a key to their final success. But against Brazil the players so nearly reverted to type. Villa's atrocious over-the-top tackle shortly after coming on as substitute for Ardiles was the most dangerous foul of a game more memorable for its unpleasantness than its football. In the end it may have served as an added incentive on the night of 21 June, for if Argentina failed against Peru, Brazil would take their place in the World Cup Final.

The 21st was an occasion for commentators to get to the ground early

Peru's man of the hour, Ramon Quiroga, their Argentinian-born goalkeeper, known as the Crazy Man (El Loco) after crash-tackling Poland's Lato near the halfway line. Here the referee books Quiroga for that extraordinary foul.

-in the afternoon, in fact, to watch Brazil's progress against Poland on television monitors and so avoid any hold-up in the massive trek to the stadium. The occasion had all the universal trappings of a 'big match': ticket touts look the same the whole world over, and they were doing profitable business in Rosario, at least with the Argentinians. Peru's support was dwindling, some of the nation's poverty reflected in the sad tale of a group who set out by road on the thousand-mile journey, got as far as Chile and then ran out of money and had to turn back. The Rosario stadium is nicknamed the Devil's Cauldron and there were to be precious few familiar voices to ease the atmosphere for the Peruvian players.

With the impeccable timing that had aided the entire television coverage of the event (until Argentina's gamesmanship in the Final) the two teams appeared shortly before 19.10 (23.10 BST) to a ticker-tape welcome of even

more fervour than usual. Peru, having built their reputation in their white strip with that red diagonal sash, looked prophetically a different side in plain red shirts and white shorts. Argentina played the 30-year-old Independiente midfield player Omar Larrosa in place of Ardiles who had not recovered from the Brazil match. Robert Wurtz from France offered a familiar face as the referee, especially to Welshmen who will not forget his penalty award that sent Scotland to Argentina instead of Wales. The Italian Sergio Gonella, who was to referee the Final, and Ferdinand Biwersi from West Germany were the linesmen.

Peru opened with a bang against Argentina and nearly put two in the home country's net. The fierce spirit of those early minutes is transmitted, centre, by Argentina's Galvan (7) and Peru's Rojas.
Opposite, below: The master-striker Mario Kempes (10) draws the ball away from Peru's Manzo (3) and prepares to shoot Argentina into a 21st-minute lead.
Below: The deed is done. Argentina lead 1–0 and scorer Kempes races back.

Four goals. Four goals. Four goals. A thought as repetitive as the drumming in the crowd. At least Argentina knew exactly what they had to do. Certainly the prevailing feeling at kick-off time was that Argentina would win, but would the margin be wide enough? The events of the opening minutes hardly led to optimism amongst the wildly cheering partisans; indeed twice their guns were nearly spiked.

Peru had charmed with their use of two wingers during the competition. Now both stumbled on the steps of glory. Munante, showing no lack of sharpness from his stomach bug, set off on a race with Passarella for a long clearance. Argentina's captain seemed

from the benches to the tunnel, surrounded by well-wishers but tall enough and dignified enough to be above it all Elsewhere in the stadium, in Rosario itself, and throughout Argentina there was bedlam . . . non-stop through the night and through the following day as well.

The cries of protest began, naturally, with the Brazilians, who interpreted the ineptitude of Peru's performance as having been 'fixed'. Nor were they the only dissenting voices I heard after the event, though significantly most of the doubters had seen the game only on television. Quiroga's always highly vulnerable position laid him open to special criticism despite the fact that he could barely be faulted with any of the goals. Moreover he had operated behind a defence hampered by a lack of fitness, a lack of experience and a lack of spirit. There were mutterings too about the refusal of Marcus Calderon, Peru's coach, to attend the obligatory post-match press conference. This was interpreted by some as an admission of complicity. But which journalist has not seen a beaten manager disappear out of a side door to avoid the pain of inquisition?

In September 1979 came allegations from Colombia that all but one of the Peruvians had accepted £25,000 each to throw the game. The source was a supposed interview with Rodolfo Manzo, but Manzo subsequently denied the accusations. Though the Brazilian authorities called for a new investigation, Joao Havelange, the president of FIFA and a Brazilian himself, dismissed the plea: 'FIFA does not have the least intention of reopening this case in any way whatsoever.' In the absence of concrete evidence I still prefer to see the manner of Peru's defeat in straightforward terms. Tired and wounded, they were mountaineers who were asked to climb one peak too many. Their swaggering skills had sustained them only for so long, and when it come to the decisive challenge their hearts were found wanting. Conversely, Argentina possessed the temperament, the discipline, the skill, and, above all, the incentive to give a dominating performance.

Back in ITV's World Cup studio Brian Clough watched a re-run of the six goals on the day of the Final itself and affirmed: 'Argentina have brought individual skills, obviously. They've

**Opposite: Luque, on the goal-line, made it 4–0 for Argentina with a diving header, and for a second Gallego (6) and Olguin (15) ignore the possibility that Peru might snatch one back. At that moment, they were on target for the Final.
Right: Quiroga made some stirring saves as the Argentinians bore down on his goal in an irresistible torrent.**

brought an exciting attacking pattern. Everybody is master of the ball throughout the team, and some of the skills near the opponents' goal are breathtaking. They've lifted their game because it's in their own particular patch. And home advantage is a tremendous advantage.'

It is now history that Argentina carried that advantage, and the skills that went with it, into the River Plate Stadium to win the World Cup. Peru returned home to a suspicious reception with the euphoria of their early form heavily diluted by their trouncing in Rosario. Several Dutch players also left Buenos Aires with the pain of the man who suffers the same nightmare twice. In 1974, and now in 1978, Holland's flowing football had missed out

on the game's greatest accolade through having to play the World Cup Final as an away match. The Dutch too would have preferred a more positive fight by Peru, reckoning a Final against even Brazil on a neutral ground preferable to taking on the host nation.

But only the partisan could quibble at the outcome. The World Cup in Argentina had always been about politics, but its political overtones were not in the end those expected or urged by the propaganda purveyors. It is not overstating the case to say that winning the competition has given Argentina a better chance of a stable existence. During our visit we were continually told that the country had never before felt so united.

A year later an enormous anniversary party included a match between Argentina and the Rest of the World. The 25th of June is the hallowed day, the date of the Final itself; but every Argentinian knows that he should also remember the 21st. That's when the cherished dream moved into the spheres of reality.

Opposite: The ticker-tape cloud rains down on the River Plate stadium in Buenos Aires in one of the most enduring images of the 1978 finals.
Below: Argentina's captain Passarella with the World Cup trophy; beside him stands Osvaldo Ardiles, shortly to grace the English game.

THE GAZETTE

BRADY AT THE LAST GASP...

Arsenal 3, Manchester United 2

THE FA CUP looked well sewn up for Arsenal as the game entered the 86th minute with the Gunners well in command. Brady had been outstanding and the score was 2-0.

But Gordon McQueen pulled one back for United and suddenly Wembley was alive again. Then there was a second eruption as Sammy McIlroy scored a brilliant equaliser. 2-2. Finally, with only seconds to extra-time, the masterful Liam Brady took over the ball. With Graham Rix in support, Arsenal yet again opened the United defence, and Alan Sunderland was on hand to slot home the winner.

Brian Talbot's opening goal for Arsenal was a puzzler in the mould of the Graham-Kelly effort in the 1971 Final, where Graham appeared to have scored but did not in fact connect with Kelly's effort which went straight in.

This time the two Arsenal men in contention were Talbot and Alan Sunderland. Either could have touched in the cross, and neither player was letting on! Cameras behind the goal gave no immediate assistance, and it wasn't until Sunday that the credit was officially awarded to Talbot.

NEWS IN BRIEF

■ Tommy Docherty moved from Derby Co to QPR.

■ George Best wanted to play for Fort Lauderdale in US but lost High Court action over his registration with Fulham. He later signed for Hibernian.

■ Peter Bonetti played his 600th game for Chelsea.

■ Alan Ball completed 100 League appearances for a club for the fourth time. He has now done it for Blackpool, Everton, Arsenal and Southampton.

Who wants to be a Millionaire?

THE TRANSFER market surged into the £1 million bracket when Forest closed their deal with Birmingham for Trevor Francis. The British record fee quickly shot up to £1,459,000, paid by Wolves to buy striker Andy Gray from Aston Villa.

Wolves were one of two clubs at the heart of these million-pound transactions. The other was Manchester City, guided by manager Malcolm Allison.

It was Allison, in fact, who set the Andy Gray deal in motion by paying £1,400,000 to Wolves in exchange for Steve Daley. Daley then became the most expensive British footballer. But not for long.

A fortnight later, Wolves moved in and completed their £1.45 million deal for Andy Gray. Despite injuries, Gray settled quickly at Wolves.

For Malcolm Allison, the Daley deal was just one of several involving massive fees.

£350,000 was paid for 17-year-old Steve McKenzie who had yet to secure a first team place at Allison's former club Crystal Palace.

Mick Robinson a promising striker for Preston in Division II went to Manchester City for £765,000.

Not that Allison had the sole rights to spending money. West Bromwich collected £900,000 from Real Madrid for Laurie Cunningham, while West Ham must have been impressed by Brian Clough's theory that Peter Shilton was worth 10 points a season to Forest. They invested £527,000 in Phil Parkes of QPR who became Britain's most expensive goalkeeper.

The pressure that these fees put on individuals is formidable. Trevor Francis, who through no fault of his own could be said to have started it all as Britain's first million-pound player, was openly anxious when he went to Forest.

But Francis soon answered his own and other people's doubts in the best possible way . . . by scoring that marvellous winner in the European Cup Final against Malmo.

IN THE GOALS

FRANK WORTHINGTON (Bolton W) led the way in Division I with 26 League and Cup goals, followed closely by Kenny Dalglish with 25.

Top marksman in the Football League was Ross Jenkins (Watford) who scored 29 times. His partnership with Luther Blissett (21 goals) gave them an astonishing League total of 50 out of the club's total of 83 goals.

In Division IV John Dungworth (Aldershot) headed the lists by some distance with 34 goals. Even so, Aldershot just missed promotion.

STOP PRESS

England qualify for European Championship Finals in Rome. Hoddle scores on debut in 2-0 win against Bulgaria at Wembley.

It was the sort of hotel that you are pleased to chance upon when the budget is tight on a family holiday. The Hotel Residence, near the centre of Munich. Functional, but with no pretensions of luxury. A reception area that merged with the lounge, upright chairs in mock leather. It was medium-range and comfortable, but no more. Not the sort of headquarters we've come to expect for a team about to play in a European Cup Final.

But Nottingham Forest and Brian Clough were here. Yet they are like no other European Cup Finalists. Throughout their four-year association they had exploded a whole almanac of football myths.

Now, on a warm Bavarian afternoon, they were preparing to fire the last salvoes. The players had already been sent to bed for what rest and sleep they would get through the waiting hours. Brian Clough and Peter Taylor were offering champagne.

Clough, newly-arrived from a family holiday in Crete, looked as tanned as an old-fashioned football. Taylor simply looked formidable. In the next two hours their talk ranged from Clough's schoolboy holidays in Blackpool – where his family went for 15 successive years and where thoughts of The Tower and comedians like Jimmy James and Frank Randall still conveyed sepia-tinted memories – to cricket and to the state of British football in the world. And to squash. Brian had sought out a court in Munich even on the morning of this Final and had lost, with no excuses, to reserve goalkeeper Chris Woods.

The match looming up in the beautiful Olympic Stadium that night was never mentioned. Yet lying beneath all the conversation and the champagne, barely disguised, was a tension that is ever-present on match days. But men who have learned to live with it have also learned how to control it.

There was no disguising the fact, though, that Nottingham Forest were crystal-clear favourites to bring the European Cup to Britain for the third successive year and follow the two victories by Liverpool. Yet it was as though Clough and Taylor sensed that, as favourites, there was somehow more to lose.

The prize was there to be taken against a Malmo side, managed by Englishman Bobby Houghton, that was modest in terms of the great European clubs and now was almost mutilated by defensive injuries.

At four o'clock the mood changed. 'It's time for work,' Clough announced briskly. 'Be back here at 6.30 and join us on the coach.' And they were gone, leaving no clue about what the work was to be.

At 6.30, an hour and three-quarters before kick-off, the coach was at the door. The Forest players were immaculate and business-like in blue blazers, ties and grey trousers. The escorting police were in uniforms of green. They, incidentally, had earlier tried in vain to advance the team's departure by half an hour. Nor were they used to being denied, except that rarely do they meet with the fortitude of men like Clough. An earlier arrival at the stadium would have given his players too much time on their hands and too much time for the wrong ideas to enter their heads. End of discussion.

The Olympic Stadium was 20 minutes distant. It was a muted journey, each player alone with his private thoughts. The players occupied the last few rows and their voices were never raised above a whisper. The barriers of apprehension were growing and nobody seemed able to break them down. Frank Clark, the oldest of them, later confirmed the atmosphere: 'We were much much more tense than usual. The players who were normally talkative were not saying a word. Others who you would expect to keep quiet now had something to say.'

Peter Taylor offered a soft drink to any who fancied it. No takers. Brian Clough jokingly chastised whoever it was who had taken his copy of the *Daily Mirror*. No response.

The spell was finally broken by an unsuspecting German. The police outriders had attracted the attention of promenading Bavarians to the coach. Now two young men began to point out the players and one was so engrossed that he walked straight into a lamp-post.

The coach erupted. The wise-cracking began. The spell was broken. And, who knows, that young German with the sore head might well have played an important role in the events of the night.

The coach drove past the barriers around the stadium, past carefully tended flower beds and lawns and into the parking place beneath this great arena. Close by were the dressing rooms; ahead a tantalizing glimpse of a corner flag and one of Europe's finest playing areas.

Once again German authority was overturned by Brian Clough. The stadium officials had orders that the teams were to be taken straight to the dressing rooms. Clough decided that his team would go straight to the pitch. He wanted them to stretch their legs and watch a junior game that was already in progress. A short, sharp discussion provided Forest with another small victory. But even now one official looked for a face-saver by trying to bar Peter Taylor's way on to the pitch. 'You have no pass,'

he growled. Taylor's withering look was just the ticket!

Forest occupied the enclosure for honoured guests–a typical gesture–while they watched the junior match. Archie Gemmill and Martin O'Neill, both having made such major contributions along the way and both now out of the side after injury, could not conceal their disappointment. Archie sat alone, hunched forward, not knowing then, but maybe suspecting it, that he had played his last competitive game for Forest (he moved to Birmingham City in that close-season).

Trevor Francis, meanwhile, could not conceal his anxiety. His boots were at his side in a supermarket plastic bag, and when he asked Clough permission to go and have a word with his parents there was a quiver on his dry lips that told its own tale. The million-pound transfer had left a frightening burden on Francis and this was his first European game for his new side.

Meanwhile Peter Taylor met briefly with Bobby Houghton of Malmo. The talk was of a possible move into English management for Houghton, who hardly seemed about to take in Taylor's down-to-earth advice. 'Go when you are most in demand . . . like now.' But Houghton's nerves were showing and, as we were to find out later, he was concealing yet another injury setback to his team.

So to the dressing rooms where most players changed briskly, where Viv Anderson, Tony Woodcock and John Robertson were gently getting the feel of the ball in the shower area, Peter Shilton was going through his rigorous

Brian Clough's expression before the match endorses Peter Taylor's account of their gruelling 1978–79 season: 'As long as six weeks before Munich we were exhausted.'

pre-match exercises and Frank Clark was sitting on the edge of the bath gently massaging more life into legs that had carried him further in the game even than he could have dreamed, and conscious also that a groin strain had only just cleared up in time to ensure his place.

Clark's appearance at Munich somehow encapsulates this remarkable Forest story. He had arrived, soon after Clough, on a free-transfer from Newcastle - a man in his thirties bent on lending what experience and professionalism he could to an ailing club. The peak of his ambition would have been to play a few more games with the dedication he had shown in over 400 for Newcastle.

But this gentle, amiable man, sitting by the bath in Munich, had, in four seasons at Forest, won a Second Division promotion place, two League Cup Final medals, a First Division championship medal and, by the end of this night, a European Cup winners' medal. To say nothing of memories to take to his dying day. Nice guys win more often than you might imagine.

Clark and Forest, and Clough and Taylor were about to complete the most astonishing and exciting upheaval of the decade. That is why this game is our choice for 1979. The 90 minutes in Munich were featureless - Francis's winning goal apart - but the years that had led up to it provide a bewildering trail of success, of imaginative management tied to unswerving principles, headlines and controversy, a run of 42 First Division matches without defeat - with only one loss in 63 competitive games - and, not least, some performances along

---

Long before he scored, the nagging runs of Francis were giving Malmo their biggest headaches.

---

the way in Europe that were at times near to perfection and at other times near to disaster.

What could have been more challenging than to have been drawn against Liverpool in the first round of the European Cup? But goals by Gary Birtles, who two years earlier was laying tiles for a living, and near to the end of the first leg by full-back Colin Barrett were enough to halt that formidable Merseyside machine.

Forest then conceded an opening goal at home against Grasshoppers of Zürich that might have unseated them - but they won 4-1 and then finished the job in Switzerland; they beat AEK of Athens and then came the thrilling switchback ride against FC Cologne that many saw as the true Final.

Here Forest were two goals down in the first leg on their own ground, a situation that defied recovery. Except that goals by Birtles, Bowyer and Robertson gave birth to that recovery and brought Forest back to 3-2, only for the Japanese Okudera, a substitute, to make it 3-3 late in the game. 'Jap Sub Sinks Forest' was the pick of the headlines next day.

It was a night when Peter Shilton came down from the heights. The man who, according to Peter Taylor, was worth 10 points a season and so was the difference between winning and losing a championship, showed himself to be flesh and blood after all.

There was perhaps a slight question mark against him when Cologne scored their first goal; there was no doubt about Okudera's third goal. It was a speculative shot without great power which Shilton, diving to his right, misjudged seriously enough for the ball to creep beneath him. Clough criticized him strongly to journalists and television cameras afterwards and Shilton blamed

himself completely for the goal.

Shilton's form throughout the tournament had been close to perfection–and particularly so when the going was fiercest in the second leg at Liverpool. Now it seemed that fate had reserved a special twist for the man who had done more than most to get Forest this far, but who might easily have blown their chance of going all the way.

But the second leg, played in Cologne, reached its crescendo when Ian Bowyer headed the only goal of the game to give Forest victory. That night Clough and Taylor sat grey and fidgeting on their touchline bench and Taylor

The goal that made the dream come true. Robertson's pinpoint cross was perfectly met by Francis, running in. The ball flew into the net over Moller's dive, and Francis landed heavily, but unhurt, beyond the goal-line.

has since spoken of that game as being the night when tension and exhaustion reached its peak in their lives:

'In Cologne I felt the blood drain from my face. Never mind about Malmo in the Final, that night in Germany was the real European Cup Final. Not many people gave us a hope of winning out there. What nobody outside the Forest dressing-room can be expected to know

is that Brian and I and all the players were mentally drained before those two matches against Cologne. Getting the lads right for the return was our major achievement of the season.

'You see, we knew that there comes a time when there's nothing more to give and our lads had just about reached that stage. We'd had about seventy competitive games by then, and as long as six weeks before Munich we were exhausted.'

So it was that Forest came back to Germany for the Final against Malmo. The Swedes had surprised Austria Wien

Opposite: Million-pound scorer Francis feels a whole lot better and receives the congratulations of Garry Birtles. Below: Tony Woodcock tries to break, but the Swedes were unyielding.

in one semi-final; Forest had beaten Cologne in the other. The hoped-for local Derby between Germany and Austria had not materialized. But with so many tickets having been sold in advance in anticipation of this neighbourly battle, the terraces were well-nigh full.

The place was alive, too, with waving red and white scarves and banners. The greatest show of support in the history of the Forest club, it came after a season when Clough had complained frequently about the lack of interest in Nottingham in their most successful team.

Malmo, in light blue, showed little that seemed capable of disturbing the Forest fans' optimism. They had come to Munich on this warm summer night without key defenders, who were

injured, and hoped to hide an even more serious disruption to their midfield. Staffan Tapper, a man with World Cup experience in 1974 and 1978, had broken a toe at the end of the last training session the previous day. He was strapped up and he gamely struggled for 34 minutes, but then signalled to Houghton, crouching on his bench, that he would have to come off.

Before this Malmo failed to accept a chance when Kenny Burns made a

Below: The 1-0 scoreline hung for an agonizingly long time over the Olympic Stadium, Munich.
Opposite: Garry Birtles, a striker of great talent who had been rescued two years earlier from a lifetime of laying tiles, could not find the touch to make it 2-0 and so guarantee Forest their victory.

mess of a back-pass and Kindvall made a more significant mess of trying to lob Peter Shilton.

On the stroke of half-time Forest scored. For the first time John Robertson found a route to the Malmo by-line – previously barred by rank after rank of Swedish defenders – and crossed to the inch for Francis. It was a cross that half-tempted Malmo's superb 'keeper Jan Moller from his line and gave Francis the opportunity to show the world his million-pound finishing.

There were no alarms for Forest after this and relatively few moments when it seemed they might add to their lead. Birtles and Woodcock both made breaks – as they did in the first half – but most times the night seemed bigger than the men.

Clough and Taylor were on their bench on the running track and, as the

huge Munich clock inched round to the last five minutes, they were engulfed by photographers. The final whistle brought a muddled but, in its way, memorable night to an end.

Clough gave his famous salute – forefinger and thumb forming a circle in the air – and he and Taylor disappeared down the tunnel and into the dressing room for a very private celebration – even before John McGovern had received the European Cup from Dr Artemio Franchi of Italy, the president of UEFA.

Forest's players went round on their lap of honour and later Clough and

Below: Malmo's spoiling tactics were calculated to prevent goals, but by repute they were still dangerous from set-pieces, and Forest were careful to respect their skills.
Opposite: John McGovern with his biggest trophy, the European Cup.

Taylor came out for their richly deserved moment. Clough was next seen upstairs in an uncomfortably crowded, hot and smoky press conference. He arrived after Houghton had got things under way by defending his team's defensive attitude and its crucial, stifling part in a disappointing night.

If Europe's Press was expecting Clough's arrival to be that of a smiling, gracious victor, they were in for a shock. He was clearly surprised by the size and formality of it – desks, microphones, lights, officials and some 200 writers – and his first words were: 'Are we on bloody trial or something?'

For a man who is usually so good at answering media questions, the conference disintegrated into a few disjointed statements unworthy of repetition. The first feeling of anti-climax was with us.

It was confirmed in the dressing-room. Players were sitting around with all the appearance of losers as though they were beginning to realize that although the prize had been won, the winning of it had brought little satisfaction to the millions who had seen it.

Peter Shilton does not entirely confirm this view: 'Forest were perfectly prepared physically and mentally and at the end of the game there was a feeling of not quite believing what we had achieved. I think that is why we were a little subdued.

'Also the players were very tired after such a long and demanding season

**Opposite: At the beginning of the Great Unwind, Trevor Francis demonstrates affection for the massive Coupe des Clubs Champions Européens.
Below: The Forest team gather round their prize.**

and I suppose there was a little disappointment at the style of the victory.'

Frank Clark, in his moment of triumph, also experienced a feeling of deflation: 'At the time it was an anticlimax and there was no real celebration afterwards. I had a quiet meal and a few drinks with Archie Gemmill. But now when I look back I get a lovely warm feeling, which goes to show that Cupties are not about how you play but about the result.'

There was also some confusion over who should have the medals. What about men like Gemmill and O'Neill who had missed out only on this night? In the end the trainer Jimmy Gordon was ordered to collect some of them in a plastic bag so that they could be distributed on the return to Nottingham.

Within half an hour the dressing room was empty. Some players-and Clough-went up the autobahn to Augsburg where their wives and families were staying. Some went to the Four Seasons Hotel in Munich for a private celebration. No fuss. No extravagant celebrations. No singing. No more shouting. The night fizzled away to nothing - though the amazing years and this final triumph can never be forgotten.

The 1970s was a decade that belonged, in domestic terms, to teams like Liverpool and Arsenal, Leeds and Manchester United. But if it belonged to one man, that man is Brian Clough. His last words to his players that night in Munich came when he stuck his head round the dressing-room door. 'What a great way to finish a season,' he said. 'Thanks a lot - I'm off.'

Off - into the 1980s.

Brian Clough looks little more cheered than he did on page 169. But the campaign is won and Peter Taylor finds enough strength to punch a last hole in the Munich sky.

So football in the '70s is now behind us and we hope we have triggered off a few memories. Perhaps, in the process, our choice and opinions have provoked a few arguments.

But looking back over the last 10 years we find it was a decade that brought about radical and, in some cases, almost unthinkable changes in our national game.

It was a decade . . . when England faltered on the world stage. In 1970 we emerged as world champions but an inexplicable defeat against West Germany in Mexico and a night of agonizing near misses against Poland at Wembley were enough to unseat Sir Alf Ramsey as manager.

It is worth suggesting, perhaps, that if England had not crumbled in the last quarter of the game against the Germans and if just one of those shots had found its way into the Polish net, Sir Alf might be England's manager today. It was surely the ultimate in fate controlling a man's career that he was lost to the game as a result of these events, and baffling that, at the end of the decade, both Sir Alf and Bobby Moore now find their livelihood away from the touchline.

Gloom overshadowed the hoped-for glory. Don Revie failed to provide the inspiration or a stable formula in his three years in the job, but Ron Greenwood has now brought a freedom and an adventure to the English game that offers optimism as we reach into the '80s.

So it was that England failed to qualify for the 1974 and 1978 World Cups and how we came in this book to reflect a decade of marking time in our national game by recalling two England matches where victory proved to be beyond our grasp.

It was a decade . . . when Scotland twice qualified for the World Cup. In Germany in 1974 they were eliminated without losing a match, but neither in this competition, nor in Argentina in 1978-and certainly in Argentina in 1978!-did they do their talents justice. Little consolation for them-except that at least they were involved in football's greatest festival while England were left on the outside looking in.'

It was a decade . . . when three leading England players moved to European clubs. Kevin Keegan overcame early problems in Hamburg to help his new club win the German championship and was himself named European Footballer of the Year; Dave Watson moved for a short period to Bremen and Laurie Cunningham to Real Madrid.

It was a trail already trodden in the '50s by John Charles and in the '60s by Jimmy Greaves, Denis Law and company, but this trading with overseas clubs spread to a new dimension when world-class players from abroad began to arrive here. Oswaldo Ardiles and Ricardo Villa came straight from Argentina's World Cup triumph to First Division action with Tottenham. The significance will not be lost on those who look into the '80s.

It was a decade . . . that saw a remarkable upswing in transfer fees. In January 1970 the record transfer fee was the £160,000 paid by Leeds United to Leicester City for the goal-snatching skills of Allan Clarke. As we leave the '70s it has stretched to £1,500,000 paid by Wolves to Aston Villa for Andy Gray, whose talents are not unrelated to Clarke's. Almost a ten-fold increase.

It was a decade . . . that started with Huddersfield Town in the First Division and Aston Villa in the Third. It ended with Huddersfield languishing in the Fourth and Villa having returned to what many claim is their rightful place in the First. In 1970 Crystal Palace were in the First Division. In a decade they slid back to the Third only to sweep once more to the First. A decade that also has ended with both Sheffield clubs, United and Wednesday, having a hard time in the Third Division. The game is no respecter of traditions.

Indeed only eight clubs who were to start the decade in the First Division remained there throughout the 10 years –Arsenal, Leeds United, Liverpool, Derby County, Coventry City, Manchester City, Everton and Ipswich Town.

It was a decade . . . where the World Cup was twice won by the host country. In 1974 the Germans overcame Holland in Munich – and the Dutch were to fall again so close to the biggest prize when they were beaten in the 1978 Final by Argentina in Buenos Aires. Brazil, who began the decade by winning the World Cup in Mexico with Pele irresistible, stumbled clumsily in 1974 and without conviction in 1978, but, like England, they face the next few years with more optimism and might well feel more at home at the 1982 tournament in Spain.

The balance of power still rests delicately between Europe and South America and there is little to suggest that that will change in the near future. The likes of El Salvador, Israel, Morocco, Zaire, Haiti, Australia, Iran and Tunisia all came to the World Cup in the '70s and learned from the experience. But they did little more than make up the numbers.

It was a decade . . . that once more had its share of cup-tie charm. We have catalogued several of the matches that produced red-blooded acts of cup-tie giant-killing and with greater emphasis on skills and coaching at lower levels in the League the gap is narrowing. So cup-tie upsets will continue to spice every season and underdog managers will continue to comfort themselves–if not attendant journalists–with the view

that 'It's eleven against eleven' and 'It's all on the day'. But they will be right.

It was a decade . . . where so much changed. But two men who didn't- and they were to skip lightly through the years–were Martin Peters and Alan Ball. They came to the '70s proudly as World Cup winners. They came to the end of those 10 years still as First Division players. If Mee and Howe, Shankly and Paisley, Clough and Taylor, Keegan and Greenwood are men who shaped the '70s, then Peters and Ball were men who survived it all with style and skill.

Surely they cannot still be there at the end of the '80s! But what shall we see then? Paisley and Greenwood will be nearing their 70th birthdays, Clough will have achieved more than enough to have satisfied himself and will be top of some other tree and Keegan's playing days will long be behind him as he counts the spoils so richly deserved.

Perhaps the new heroes will come from North America. At this time we are deafened by their razmatazz, but beneath it all we are told of millions in the schools making preparations for a mighty explosion; many more coaches will be needed to point those youngsters in the right direction. Cool heads and stable administration are called for in America to go with their undoubted marketing gifts.

Will America be a world power by 1990? They have bent the laws to suit their own requirements–a 35-yard offside line and a shoot-out to prevent a match ending level–and they will now need to bend themselves in coming years to conform to world standards. And are the owners–the real power men –genuinely interested in the game of football? How long-term is their thinking? In the '80s we shall find out as the football world continues to look in their direction.

In Britain each bad winter will lead to the cry for summer football. We believe its advantages are worthy of intense investigation if the needs of the football public are to be properly satisfied. The appeal of a family outing on a summer evening is undeniable; the arguments against it - the clash with cricket, tradition, the finals of European competitions and World Cups - are formidable.

In 1990 we shall be writing about the same argument. Just as we shall be trumpeting still the need for all-seater stadia. The trend is for clubs to reduce capacity by installing more seats as the football public goes looking for - and insisting on - a greater degree of Satur-day afternoon comfort. Aberdeen led the way with just such a stadium in the '70s - only a few will find the cash to follow the pattern in the coming decade.

That is because the escalating transfer market will continue to bite deep into every club's financial reserves. To think that we started the '70s with Allan Clarke's £160,000 transfer big enough to set the heads wagging, only to end it with £1,500,000 being the fee to tempt Andy Gray to Wolves. If that rate of increase were to continue through the next decade some 13-year-old schoolboy now performing on a remote playing field would, in 1989, be transferred for £15,000,000! But that's another story.

Page numbers in *italics* refer to illustrations.